FROM STUDENT TO SOLICITOR

*The Complete Guide to Securing a
Training Contract*

First Edition

Charlotte Harrison

SWEET & MAXWELL   THOMSON REUTERS

First Edition 2010

Published in 2010 by Thomson Reuters (Legal) Limited
(Registered in England & Wales, Company No 1679046.
Registered Office and address for service:
100 Avenue Road, London, NW3 3PF) trading as Sweet & Maxwell

For further information on our products and services, visit
www.sweetandmaxwell.co.uk

Printed in the UK by CPI William Clowes, Beccles, NR34 7TL
Typeset by Interactive Sciences Ltd, Gloucester

No natural forests were destroyed to make this product;
only farmed timber was used and re-planted.

British Library Cataloguing in Publication Data

A CIP catalogue record for this book
is available from the British Library

ISBN 978–1–847–03956–9

FOREWORD

To be a solicitor means more than to be a member of a profession. The badge of solicitor is synonymous not only with great technical and legal expertise, but also with honour, integrity and authority. Few professions can boast such a rich variety of disciplines, occupations and opportunities, and fewer still can claim to be as rewarding or intellectually challenging. With so many options available, there is more to consider than ever before making important decisions about your career.

As we enter the second decade of the 21st century, the solicitors' profession moves from strength to strength. The last ten years have seen an unprecedented level of change and the opening up of new avenues for new entrants to discover and explore. Whereas once a solicitor would expect to follow a traditional path through private practice, they can now opt to argue in the courts as a solicitor advocate or to pursue a path as an in-house adviser in industry or government. In addition, more and more solicitors are choosing to exercise their abilities overseas.

However, greater opportunity does not mean a lessening of competition. A great many candidates vie for the same training contracts each year and it is essential to have both eyes open to the challenge ahead. This volume contains a great many valuable hints and tips for all aspiring solicitors and I am sure that it will prove to be of real worth to all who follow its advice.

The Law Society is also committed to assisting all aspirant members of the profession to reach their potential. The Society's Junior Lawyers Division is free to join and provides support for students and for young solicitors in the early stages of the careers. I encourage all readers to take full advantage of the information and advice available to them before deciding which path they wish to take.

I wish you every success as you embark on your new career.

Robert Heslett
President of the Law Society of England and Wales

FOREWORD

DEDICATION

This book is dedicated to my parents
Vicki and Patrick Harold-Harrison

ACKNOWLEDGEMENTS

I owe a huge debt to the lawyers, graduate recruitment mangers, students, and tutors who contributed to this project; your voices have brought the work to life.

Kelvin Balmont, Matthew Barker, Glenn Beavis, Nicholas Bennett, Elizabeth Bradley, Alexander Brown, Rebecca Brown, Caroline Burt, Simon Camilleri, Moira Campbell, Sean Campbell, Kevin Chard, Philippa Chatterton, Sibylle Cheruvier, Amanda Danvers, Anna Douglass, Lynn Ford, Elena Gubay, Mark Heath, Robert Heslett, Angela Ingram, Kerry James, Cheryl Keal, Michael Kelley, James King, Thomas Moore, Kelly Myles, Linda Lee, Sam Lee, Veronica Oldfield, Malcolm Padgett, Nick Page, Jo Pennick, Jonathan Pugh-Smith, Clare Reeve, Sarita Riley, Lorna Sansom, Christopher Skinner, Danielle Spalding, Tom Storey, Sally Tattersfield, Nitish Upadhyaya, Jennifer Walker, Claire Walls, Ben Wheeler, Rachael Williams, and Oi-Yuyn Wong.

I am grateful to Maebh Harding, James Harold-Harrison, Kerry James, Lee Roach, Julie Skinner and Gilliane Williams for taking the time to review draft chapters for me and for making such helpful comments and suggestions.

Thanks must, of course, go to everyone at Sweet & Maxwell who was involved in the production of this book. In particular, I am grateful to Constance Sutherland for her support, advice and patience (even when my son, Patrick, made his arrival into the world three months before the final deadline with one section still to go!). You have made my first experience of the publishing process a most enjoyable one.

I am grateful to Bill Cole from the Research Unit of the Law Society for allowing me to use extracts from his reports on Trends in the Solicitors' Profession (Annual Statistical Reports 2007 and 2008).

Thank you to my sister, Annabelle, for encouraging me through the weeks when I thought the writing would never end, and to my godmother, Theresa Wride, for all your help and support in the final weeks of this project—I would never have finished it without you.

Of course, I could not finish without acknowledging my parents who have always supported and encouraged me unwaveringly, and have sacrificed so much along the way. This book is dedicated to you both with much love.

Finally, thank you to my husband, Ian, for encouraging me to take on this project and, as always, for supporting me through to the very end. We have so much to look forward to and there is no one I would rather share the journey with.

CONTENTS

SECTION 1: A CAREER AS A SOLICITOR

1 WHY BECOME A SOLICITOR?

By Linda Lee, Vice President of the Law Society

Of all of the questions that I've ever been asked, this is probably the easiest to answer. If you want a career which is mentally stimulating, personally challenging and is fundamental to the workings of a civilised society then you should become a solicitor.

The profession has grown in recent years and is far more diverse than ever before. Many solicitors still work in a traditional high street practice, but it is no longer the default career option that it once was. Private practice also encompasses multinational firms and many solicitors work overseas. There are also far more opportunities to work outside the traditional private practice model. Today, one in four solicitors work in-house, in business or in local and central government. Solicitors can now qualify to have exactly the same rights of audience as barristers and represent clients in all courts. Far more solicitors are entering the judiciary at all levels and recently Lord Collins, a former solicitor, was appointed as one of the first justices of the Supreme Court.

Our society is built on the rule of law, but the law is a complex thing. A solicitor is an enabler—a person who helps others to untangle the complexities of the legal system. In doing so the solicitor empowers individuals, businesses and other organisations to take best advantage of the provisions of the law.

Solicitors are able to help in a myriad of circumstances, from the certification of mundane transactions to navigating the labyrinth of business tax law, or ensuring that an individual's dying wishes are carried out in the manner that that person intended. Solicitors are also able to help individuals level the playing field in disputes with the state and to protect rights and enforce obligations. Every day, solicitors ensure that this is a just land where justice is available to the ordinary citizen, particularly through the provision of publicly funded work.

Yet a solicitor is more than simply an expert on the law—he or she is often a trusted adviser. Due to the sensitivity and gravity of many of the issues on which solicitors are asked to work, it is vital that they should offer support to their clients at a time of great pressure and vulnerability. A solicitor provides not only a legal mind, but a supporting arm and a human face.

Being a solicitor is more than just a job. It is a vocation which makes many demands on an individual. Because the workings of the English legal system rely on the integrity of solicitors and on their undertakings, solicitors are required to operate to the very highest ethical standards.

An increasingly large proportion of solicitors are employed directly by organisations to provide in-house legal advice. Aside from providing an essential legal reference point, in-house solicitors act as a valuable moral compass. Whereas the head of a business might have shareholders as his or her first priority, every solicitor is bound to uphold the rule of law as a professional obligation. Regardless of whether they work for businesses, local or central government or even the military, solicitors protect the reputations of some of the world's most important brands and shape the ethical standards of their organisations. They offer not only the benefit of their knowledge, but also their integrity.

Solicitors are role models in their communities. They are often relied upon to act for the public good without payment (also known as pro bono work). For example, some solicitors take on cases without charge or act as unpaid trustees of charities or non executive directors and governors of educational establishments.

For my part, it is only 16 years since I qualified. I was aged 30 and had three children and I well remember the uncertainty I felt at the start of my career. Initially I thought I wanted a career in commercial law, but I realised that I gained far more personal satisfaction from representing individuals. Therefore I developed a career in clinical negligence and coronial law.

It is a career which has given me great personal satisfaction. I have been able to help many sick and injured people receive just compensation after a devastating injury and to free them from the worry as to how they will purchase the medical treatment and aids they need to lead a normal life. I hope that some of my work, particularly in the coroners' court, has enabled lives to be saved and injuries avoided because of the spotlight the investigations have thrown on problems in healthcare provision. I had the privilege to be able to use that knowledge and those skills to work in-house for two years for a charity dedicated to patient safety.

The path that I took is not the path for everyone, but the variety of options is so broad that I am certain that there will be a path for you. Whichever direction you choose will be hugely competitive with no guarantee of success. It is not for the faint hearted and not all will succeed. However, in spite of the difficulties along the way, I have never regretted making the decision to enter this profession. I hope that one day you are able to look back and feel the same.

2 THE VIEW FROM THE TOP

Malcolm Padgett, Recruitment Partner, Coffin Mew LLP

I became a solicitor for a, probably *not*, very good reason—my father was one!

Having said that, I believe that anybody considering the solicitors' profession must make sure they know exactly what the career (and business of law firms) really entails in practice. My family firm provided me with plenty of "work experience", on reception, storing deeds or even painting offices—but I do not recall my father letting me near any legal work!

Work experience is a crucial part of making the right career choice, but it is difficult to obtain. In my role as Recruitment Partner I am just as impressed by work experience obtained by prospective trainees within the administration and support functions of a variety of legal environments as I am with exposure to fee earning—good lawyers need to understand their business from top to bottom.

Whilst the family firm was small, and focused on private clients, at Oxford University I found myself being firmly pointed towards London and what would now be called the "Magic Circle". I therefore (more by circumstance than dynamic career choice) trained with, and then spent 10 very happy years working as a solicitor for, a major London firm in an environment a long way (in every sense) from our family firm. Since my first day there involved meeting one of the Beatles and, thereafter, I acted for world renowned companies in markets as diverse as cosmetics and hamburgers, how could I ever argue against a young person choosing to commence their career in London?

I am not there now however—and have not been there for over 25 years. Why?

Once I had a family of my own, and when it became time to consider partnership, I realised that my background, and the original reason why I became a solicitor, was rooted in the relationship between home and work—and that the two *had* to compliment each other. I have therefore spent the remainder of my career as a partner in a mid sized regional firm, still handling top quality work but living just ten minutes from the office.

The moral is, I think, to understand where your core motivations lie; when you are starting out take the best opportunities available but be careful to end up where your heart truly lies.

Elizabeth Bradley, Corporate Tax Partner, Berwin Leighton Paisner LLP

I qualified as a corporate tax solicitor at Berwin Leighton Paisner in September 2001. I advise in all areas of corporate tax, for example, mergers and acquisitions and corporate reorganisations, and also on real estate related tax issues including capital allowances, VAT and stamp duty land tax, property development and investment for residents and non-residents, property joint ventures and property funds.

Very few people have a burning ambition to become a tax specialist at an early age! Perhaps more people should because tax is not dry and bookish. Tax brings you into contact with every area of legal practice. Corporation tax is the driver of most corporate finance and property transactions as it often the area of law which adds value to transactions if they are structured in a tax-efficient manner.

I chose to become a City tax solicitor due to the intellectually challenging nature of the work. I enjoy working closely with clients on a daily basis in order to deliver practical, innovative and commercial solutions to their problems. It is crucial to develop a close relationship with your clients in order to understand their business needs.

A City solicitor is, in the long term, a profession which rewards hard work, commitment and drive. I decided to pursue a career in this field at an early age and embarked on several vacation placements at different law firms in order to experience life as a City solicitor. Securing a training contract can be difficult and very competitive. However, it is often true to say that most difficult things in life worth achieving are those things worth having!

Mark Heath, Solicitor to the Council, Southampton City Council

I was fortunate when I was at school to have outstanding career advice and made a decision while I was doing my 'A' Levels that a career in law was the route I wished to take. I was also fortunate enough to end up at my first choice university and they had a lunch time slot where practising solicitors or trainee solicitors from various sectors came in and spoke about their careers to help and encourage the law undergraduates in terms of their own career choices.

I can still remember the session from the local government trainee solicitor who talked about actively being involved in court cases and presenting them on behalf of the local authority whilst still a trainee solicitor, and indicated that he was carrying a significant workload: in essence he was being trained by being thrown in at the deep end. It was this that clicked with me, and it was on this basis that I ended up applying to work in local government, starting my career at Hampshire County Council and then moving to Southampton City Council.

So what is life like in local government for a solicitor? We usually consider ourselves to have one and only one client which obviously sets us apart from our private sector colleagues, but my client spends £1bn a year, employs 9,000 people and touches every citizen's life on a daily basis in the city. We undertake almost every sphere of standard legal work as well as the specialist areas required in local government. We also, particularly at a more senior level, have direct interface with councillors. That political interface, and all that goes with it, is a significant issue which the corporate legal advisor at a senior level in a local authority has to develop.

So when advising an aspiring law student about a career in local government, I would say don't believe everything you read about life in the public sector. It is hard work, there are major demands, and you will not get any benefits that you would not get in the private sector. What you will get is a very rewarding job; indeed you will probably find yourself doing things that your counterparts in the private sector cannot do because of the status of local government, e.g. appearing in court in minor matters before you are admitted. If you stay in local government you will find that the career path provides you with a broad range of opportunities, for example specialising in a particular area of law to develop greater expertise, moving into management, or becoming a policy advisor.

Finally, there is still something about the public service ethos that should not be discounted. Some aspects of the work bring it out more than others. For example, I am a Returning Officer for elections. In conducting elections I am making sure that the electorate have the right to determine who governs them and that the democratic process is properly and effectively implemented. Undertaking roles like that provides an enormous degree of personal satisfaction, and so I believe that the public service ethos remains a powerful factor in seeing the public sector as a good career choice.

Nick Page, Chairman, Bond Pearce LLP

Those who truly reach the top of the profession are those who are viewed by their peers as being outstanding lawyers in the specialist area of the law in which they chose to practise. Very few of us can achieve that status. But one of the best things about becoming a lawyer is that we determine the direction of our careers and can set our own goals and challenges. Most lawyers are motivated by giving legal advice. However some of us decide that we would like new challenges and step forward to learn how to lead, manage and develop our firms in increasingly competitive environments. We are then privileged to be appointed a Managing Partner or, like me, to be elected by our partners as their Senior Partner or Chairman.

As lawyers we get immense pleasure from receiving thanks from clients when we achieve a particular result for them, whether it is the sale of their business, a defence of a difficult claim or even the completion of a complex transaction following months of negotiation. We are also rewarded by coming up with innovative solutions for our clients, winning new work and, of course, attracting new clients. Those who take on management roles, receive satisfaction from seeing their firm fulfil its stated vision, achieve its goals and to see the firm going from strength to strength.

It is immensely rewarding to build your own client base and to find people respecting your advice as you assist them in achieving their goals or overcoming their problems. It is also a pleasure to work with people of like minds, who thrive on intellectual challenges, and to work within a culture of a firm which matches your own aspirations and ambition.

I now sit, with our Managing Partner, Victor Tettmar, as joint head of a successful and well respected law firm after 28 years as a solicitor. For most of my working life I have advised companies and businessmen on corporate work, mergers and acquisitions, commercial agreements and more latterly specialising in competition law. I am fortunate that I have dealt with many gifted businessmen from various walks of life who, for the most part, I have really enjoyed working with. Today I am faced with different challenges which are equally rewarding, such as providing the strategic direction for a firm that has changed significantly from where it started in Plymouth in the 1870's; the most rapid change coming in the past 20 years.

Most of us like to keep our "hands in" as lawyers and to remain close to the clients with whom we have developed great working relationships over the years. Now I can use my experience to put "the commercial spin" on often immensely complicated legal and economic competition law problems which are being solved by the great team that I have gathered around me. It is still very satisfying to win a new client or a good piece of work from time to time.

When entering the profession, you should keep your options open, take the opportunities that are offered to you, and always remember that a career in the law offers a diverse range of practice areas and many different directions in which you may turn. Most importantly, early on in your career, try to experience as many areas of the law as possible and to build your experience. You will come to identify where you feel most comfortable, not only in understanding the nuances of the legal advice that you are giving, but also the types of client you feel you should be advising. If you are lucky and, of course, work hard, you will be able to choose the area of law in which you practise and the type of clients you wish to act for.

What is crucially important is to have a career that gives you personal satisfaction from achieving your own goals and to judge your career by far more than your earnings. Nowadays we operate in an increasingly transparent world and it is very easy to compare your monetary rewards with those obtained by other people in the profession. However, it would be wrong to rely on this as a measure of your individual success.

Make clear choices as to the direction in which you want to take your career; create and then seize the opportunities that come your way; and don't be afraid to change course if you are not happy with what you are achieving. There are many different types of firms and clients and areas of the law in which to specialise. The law is a fantastic environment in which to have a rewarding and challenging career. Make the most of it!

Michael Kelley, Former District Solicitor, Chichester District Council

After qualifying as a solicitor I progressed through the posts of Assistant Solicitor, Senior Solicitor, Principal Solicitor and then District Solicitor for a local authority. As District Solicitor I was the chief legal adviser to a local authority with a diverse range of functions. I was the corporate legal adviser to councillors, chief officers and other professional staff, and was the manager of nine other solicitors, legal executives and support staff. The legal team was seen as fulfilling an essential support role to a wide range of other professional council staff such as planners, environmental health officers, housing officers and engineers.

My work included giving corporate legal advice and dealing with major litigation, council and board meetings, and the ethical standards of conduct of councillors. I also gave support and guidance to the legal staff on areas such as litigation, conveyancing, contracts, enforcement, housing and leisure services.

Any student who is interested in local government work should be prepared to be versatile, to be willing to take on new challenges, to keep up to date with the ever changing law, to work extra hours to meet your deadlines, to be co-operative with staff at all levels and professions, and to enjoy the variety of work which a major local authority can give.

To be an effective senior local government lawyer, you may need to keep up to date with a range of general law topics such as litigation, conveyancing and contract law as well as specialist local government law areas. A good knowledge of the legislation relating to human rights, data protection and freedom of information is also important in the public sector. You should also be prepared for the challenge of constantly working towards deadlines for meetings and court work, dealing with other professions inside and outside local government, dealing with the public, and accept the fact that your work may be subject to scrutiny by councillors, the press, the district auditor and other government agencies.

Although I have always worked for local authorities I have spoken to solicitors who have joined local government from private practice and they have been impressed by the intellectual satisfaction which you can obtain in local government from dealing with services which really matter to the public, the constantly changing rules and regulations which govern the public sector, and the opportunity for responsibility to be given to lawyers early in their careers.

Glenn Beavis, Former Senior Legal Counsel, Shell International
Limited, and Racing Driver Manager

Law is a great profession. It can provide many things—interesting work, the opportunity to meet fascinating people, and the opportunity to travel and to make a difference by being yourself. It has everything that a soap opera has, plus a bit more—politics, power struggles and eccentrics. It is a very diverse profession indeed.

For me, being a solicitor is most rewarding when you can make a difference, particularly if you have a client who is not in a strong position and through your knowledge and the right approach and tactics you are able to improve their position.

My position in-house took me all over the world and enabled me to work on projects that really make a difference to the way people live their lives. The breadth and depth of the legal knowledge of the colleagues I worked with was very impressive.

Because of the diversity of the legal profession, as a solicitor you have many options open to you as to where to work. The common general divide is between working in private practice and working in-house. There are however many different companies and organisations that fall under the banner of 'in-house'—from multinational companies, to charities and universities. Being a solicitor in-house undoubtedly brings you closer to the heart of the organisation you represent. For many solicitors in private practice who move in-house, this can be very refreshing because you are in at the beginning of a matter and integral to it, helping to shape things as they evolve.

Many solicitors that I know who have tasted the life of an in-house solicitor do not wish to return to private practice. Not because private practice is bad, but because being in-house is different in a way that cannot be replicated in a law firm. Depending where you work, it can provide more balance to your days. I would certainly recommend that you try a spell in-house and see what you think. If you are not sure about making the step away from a law firm, you could try and arrange a secondment to a company or organisation that is a client of the firm you work at, if such an arrangement is available.

It is hard work qualifying as a solicitor. It is also expensive and often there is no guarantee of a job at the end, which can be daunting. But for every 10 jobs you may apply for and not get, you only need one to say yes. If you are committed, you will succeed and you can make a difference. The key is never to give up trying, not ever.

Because qualifying as a solicitor is a hard slog at times, you will inevitably have moments when you question whether it is all worth it. It is worth it though, whatever you choose to do once you qualify. Even if you choose to step outside of the legal profession, the skills you will have learnt and taken on board will serve you very well wherever you end up.

I chose to step outside of the legal profession and set up as a manager of racing drivers. Not something that you will hear many legal career advisors talk about! The point here though is that my legal background serves me very well in my chosen profession. Work hard, qualify, get some experience under your belt and then ask yourself, "What do I really enjoy doing?"; with the skill set you have acquired, go and do it.

SECTION 2: FIRST STEPS TO PRACTICE

3 TIME FOR A REALITY CHECK

In 2008, 7,606 students passed the LPC but only 6,012 new traineeships were registered in the year ending July 31, 2007 and 6,303 in the year ending July 31, 2008.

Sources: Trends in the Solicitors' Profession. Annual Statistical Report 2008, pp.35 and 37, and Trends in the Solicitors' Profession. Annual Statistical Report 2007, p.6, prepared by Bill Cole, Research Unit of the Law Society.

Qualifying as a solicitor can mark the beginning of a rewarding career, but it is important to be aware of the challenges ahead before you embark on the rigorous recruitment process. The competition is fierce, the work can be incredibly demanding, and the field is full of exceptional players. Are you really prepared for the challenge?

Applying for training contracts can be a very demoralising process and it does really test how much you want to do this. People don't appreciate how much work you're going to have to do just to get one interview. Before you even start, you almost have to say, "I'm just going to keep doing this however long it takes".

A Trainee Solicitor

4 WHAT SORT OF SOLICITOR WILL YOU BE?

74.1% of solicitors holding practising certificates work in private practice; the remainder work mainly in commerce and industry and the public sector.

Source: Trends in the Solicitors' Profession. Annual Statistical Report 2008, p.5, prepared by Bill Cole, Research Unit of the Law Society

Perhaps one of the most appealing aspects of the solicitors' profession is that it is a very broad church offering a wide variety of opportunities. The key to a successful and fulfilling career is choosing an area of law and type of working environment that best suits your personality, skills, and lifestyle. It probably goes without saying that the life of a market town property lawyer is a world away from the life of a City banking lawyer or a publicly funded criminal defence lawyer and, while each has its own unique rewards and challenges, what is most important is that you follow the right path for you, not the one that offers the greatest financial incentives or will most impress your family and friends.

Section 5 discusses the different areas of legal practice, and provides commentary on the different types of law firm and other employers in the legal sector. For now, it is enough to say that solicitors' practice areas can be broadly divided into three categories: commercial work; private client work; and public work. As you would imagine, solicitors involved in commercial practice tend to deal with corporate clients who need business-related advice (e.g. commercial contracts, mergers and acquisitions, intellectual property, corporate tax, and commercial property transactions) while private client solicitors deal with individual clients helping them with legal issues relating to their private affairs (e.g. personal taxation, residential property transactions, divorce, or personal injury claims). Public work includes criminal defence or prosecution work, judicial review cases, and immigration matters. It is also important to realise that you do not have to work for a firm of solicitors in private practice. Solicitors can also work as 'in-house' lawyers within companies, not-for-profit organisations, local authorities, Central Government, or the Crown Prosecution Service.

Given the breadth of practice areas and training opportunities available, you must engage in thorough and timely research and honest reflection before you even consider applying for training contracts. This is important on two counts: first, it will help you make an informed decision about whether this is really the career for you; and, secondly, it will help you decide which of the many and varied practice areas you would be most suited to. If you are honest with yourself and get this research right, you will greatly improve your chances of securing a training contract and, crucially, of enjoying a long and satisfying career.

5 YOUR PATH TO PRACTICE

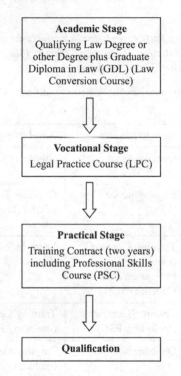

Academic Stage

Qualifying Law Degree or other Degree plus Graduate Diploma in Law (GDL) (Law Conversion Course)

Vocational Stage

Legal Practice Course (LPC)

Practical Stage

Training Contract (two years) including Professional Skills Course (PSC)

Qualification

Figure 1

As Figure 1 illustrates, you do not necessarily have to study law at university in order to qualify as a solicitor, although the route to qualification is quicker and cheaper for those with a qualifying law degree because they do not have to spend an extra year taking a law conversion course.

> **Note:** *a qualifying law degree is one that covers the core legal subjects required by the Solicitors Regulation Authority (SRA). See s.3 for more information on qualifying law degrees.*

The chart below summarises the route to qualification for both law and non-law graduates.

Year	Law graduates	Non-law graduates
1–3	Qualifying law degree course	Other degree course
4	Legal Practice Course (LPC)	Graduate Diploma in Law (GDL) (law conversion course)
5	Training Contract (including Professional Skills Course (PSC))	Legal Practice Course (LPC)
6	Training Contract (including PSC)	Training Contract (including PSC)
7	Qualification	Training Contract (including PSC)
8		Qualification

It is also possible to complete each of the GDL and LPC on a part time basis over two years. This can be useful for students who need to combine the course with paid work to fund their studies, or those who have not secured a training contract and wish to enhance their CV with legal work experience while studying.

The Recruitment Timetable

The competition for graduate jobs in the legal profession is increasing rapidly. It is therefore important to ensure that you stand out from the crowd. This can be achieved by developing your CV as soon as you start university; don't wait until you've graduated (it might be too late!). Getting involved in university competitions, pro bono activities and, most importantly of all, gaining a wide variety of work experience are things that recruiters will expect to see on your applications. By being organised and starting your research early, this can be achieved whilst getting good marks in your assessments. You don't have to get involved in every single activity that comes your way, perhaps try and do one every semester.

Tom Storey, Third Year Law Undergraduate, University of Portsmouth

Students need to be aware of the recruitment process at a very early stage because it will alert them to the importance of work experience. They really need to be trying to get as much legal experience or exposure to the legal world (which can include court visits, etc.) as early as possible and at the same time learn about what's ahead of them in terms of the route to becoming a solicitor.

Veronica Oldfield, Careers Consultant and Tutor, College of Law

This timetable provides suggestions for activities that will enhance your CV and gives advice on when to conduct your research and how to prepare effectively for the application process. To ensure that you do not miss important deadlines in the application process, it should be read in conjunction with the specific timetables provided by law careers websites such as *www.lawcareers.net* or the Student's Guide to Becoming a Lawyer (Chambers & Partners).

First year law and second year non-law undergraduates

- Get as much legal work experience as you can and make the most of any contacts within the legal profession.

- Participate in as many client interviewing competitions, negotiating competitions, court visits, mock trials and moots as you can without compromising your studies (if your university does not have these initiatives in place, speak to your Student Law Society or tutors, or consider establishing one yourself).

- Attend careers fairs and any guest lectures or careers workshops to find out as much as possible about the recruitment process, the different areas of legal practice, and the breadth of training opportunities that are available to you. It is important to get this preparation out the way this year to put yourself in the best possible position when the recruitment process starts in earnest next year. Never miss an opportunity to make a new contact and always invest time in following them up.

- Consider volunteering at your local Citizens Advice Bureaux or Trading Standards office. Your university might run a clinical legal education programme offering such training schemes. If not, get in touch with your local office to find out about volunteering opportunities.

- Find out about, and get involved in, any other pro bono initiatives at your university (see s.4 for more information on pro bono initiatives).

- Use your long summer holiday wisely to gain as much experience as possible to enhance your CV. This is particularly important this summer as you are likely to be applying for training contracts next year and will need all the ammunition you can find when it comes to tackling the tricky questions on application forms.

- Consider getting involved in charity work or fundraising events. This is a great way to develop key skills such as teamwork, negotiation and communication, and it will give you something interesting to talk about at interviews. This experience is likely to be particularly useful if you are interested in public legal work as employers will be looking for candidates who have shown a genuine interest in helping people and can demonstrate a commitment to their community or a particular cause.

- Make a serious commitment to researching the legal recruitment process, and the breadth of opportunities available within the profession, so that you can start making informed decisions about which career path you would like to follow (see s.6).

- Visit your university careers centre and get to know the careers advisors. They are an invaluable source of help so it is worth getting in touch with them as early as possible, rather than waiting until the busy periods when everyone else is also desperate for advice.

I got most of my information about the recruitment process during the first year of my degree from the vocational events that my Student Law Society put on. I even went along to a lot of the second year events so I had an idea of what I had to work up to. The vocational events included guest lectures, application workshops, commercial awareness training, networking drinks receptions, and law fairs.

Jo Pennick, Third Year Law Undergraduate, King's College London

Second year law and third year non-law undergraduates

- Continue to follow last year's advice (as appropriate) although by now you should have made some decisions about your chosen career path and therefore your research and networking should become more targeted.

- At the beginning of the year, list the key deadlines in the recruitment calendar and the dates of any important careers related events (these are usually available from legal careers websites and/or your university careers centre).

- Continue to participate in pro bono initiatives.

- Apply for vacation schemes and training contracts (check deadlines for each firm).

- Talk to students who have already secured a training contract and ask them to review and provide feedback on your CV and application forms.

- Attend mock interviews and assessment centre workshops at your university careers centre.

- Some law schools and university careers centres maintain electronic or paper based databases where you can review feedback forms from students who have attended interviews at particular firms. This is an excellent form of preparation and should give you a clearer idea of what to expect from the interview and a better understanding of what that firm is looking for in prospective trainees.

- Collect prospectuses and attend law school open days to find out more about the LPC/GDL.
- Non-law undergraduates should apply for a place on the GDL.

Third year law undergraduates and GDL students who have not already secured a training contract

- Continue to follow last year's advice (as appropriate).
- Collect prospectuses and visit law school open days to find out more about the LPC.
- Apply for a place on the LPC. If you are concerned about embarking on the course without a training contract, get in touch with someone from your chosen provider and ask about the percentage of students who join without a training contract and how many secure one before completing the course.
- Continue to apply for vacation schemes and training contracts. Seek feedback if you are unsuccessful and take full advantage of the support available from your careers service.
- Apply for student membership of the Solicitors Regulation Authority (SRA).
- Find out whether your university or law school operates a formal or informal mentoring programme to enable you to learn from other people's experiences and make some useful contacts within the profession.

LPC students who have not already secured a training contract

- Continue to follow last year's advice (as appropriate).
- Critically review your CV, application forms and interview performance. Seek advice from careers advisors, friends, or tutors as they might pick up on weaknesses that you have missed.

Start applying for training contracts as early as possible. You learn something from each round of applications that you do and if you are not successful you can apply again the next year. Law firms have specific recruitment periods and they generally recruit two years in advance so you need to apply early.

Rachael Williams, Solicitor, Coffin Mew LLP

SECTION 3: TRAINING

6 THE SEVEN FOUNDATIONS OF LEGAL KNOWLEDGE

The Solicitors Regulation Authority (SRA) (the body that is responsible for regulating the conduct and training of solicitors in England and Wales) requires that in order to complete the academic stage of training to become a solicitor, a student must cover certain core subjects. These subjects are known collectively as the "seven foundations of legal knowledge". In addition, students must receive training in legal research.

The Foundation Subjects

- Criminal Law.
- Law of the European Union.
- Obligations 1 (Contract Law).
- Obligations 2 (Tort Law).
- Land Law.
- Equity and Trusts.
- Public Law (Constitutional, Administrative, and Human Rights Law).

Law conversion courses cover the seven compulsory foundation subjects, as well as providing an introduction to the English legal system and the general skills required for legal study. Qualifying law degrees combine the same foundation and legal skills subjects with opportunities to explore specialist units such as intellectual property law, commercial law, health care law, or company law.

The foundation subjects lay down the basic principles upon which other specialist areas of law are built. For example, contract law is an important and interesting subject in its own right, but it also provides the basis of other specialist areas such as employment law, commercial law, and construction law. It is therefore best to avoid thinking of each subject as a separate, compartmentalised body of knowledge. It is equally important to realise that real life is rarely as straightforward as the neatly packaged scenarios that are found inside undergraduate law exam papers. Thus, a "real life" legal problem is unlikely to consist of a single issue and might well involve elements of, for example, tort, contract, and land law. The trick for the lawyer is to unravel, and make sense of, the various strands and decide which ones hold the key to achieving the client's aims.

What will I study?

The key features of each of the foundation subjects are summarised below. As you will realise when you embark on your legal studies, these descriptions are somewhat over simplified but serve their purpose in this particular context.

Criminal Law is the study of criminal offences and related punishments. Imagine that you represent Sheila, a 26 year old woman who has been married to Paul for six months. During that time, Paul has repeatedly beaten and mentally abused her. She is too frightened to tell anyone, but dreams about having the strength to kill him to make it all stop. One evening, Paul is asleep in the chair after drinking several bottles of cider and Sheila stabs him to death with a large kitchen knife. Is Sheila guilty of murder? Are any defences available to her? Does it matter that she was not actually in any immediate danger at the time she killed her husband?

Law of the European Union is the study of the formation and government of the European Union and the relationships between its Member States. Imagine that you represent the British Government. British fishermen are angry because Spanish fishermen are fishing in British waters (using UK companies to purchase the vessels) to avoid fishing quotas. The British Government has passed a piece of legislation to prevent such activity by requiring that 75 per cent of directors and shareholders of such companies must be British. Will this legislation be contrary to European Union Law? Could the Spanish Government take legal action to stop the new ownership rules?

Obligations 1 (Contract) is the study of the law governing agreements made between two or more legal persons. Imagine that you represent Julie Jones, a well known cat breeder. Julie's favourite cat has just given birth to a litter of kittens so Julie places a bulk order of cat food with her usual supplier. She is in a hurry and doesn't bother to read the terms and conditions when she signs the order form. If she had read them, she would have found a clause excluding any liability for loss or damage caused by the company's products. Two weeks after she starts to use the new cat food, the kittens develop a nasty sickness bug and within another week four of them are dead. Tests reveal that the cat food contained lethal quantities of a toxic substance. Can Julie sue the supplier for breach of contract? What is the effect of the exclusion clause? Does it matter whether Julie purchased the food in a domestic or business capacity?

Obligations 2 (Tort) is the study of certain civil wrongs and includes actions such as negligence, nuisance, and defamation. The injured or wronged party may be granted a remedy, usually via an award of money (damages), which will seek to compensate him for the loss sustained. Imagine that you act for Brian Smith, a keen dog walker. One Sunday afternoon, on his way back from a long walk with the dogs, Brian is forced to wait at the railway crossing while a train passes. Shortly after it passes through the station, there is a terrible crash. Brian runs to the scene to see if he can help but there is nothing he can do. Brian has been suffering from severe depression for three months as a result of the carnage and terrible injuries that he witnessed. He is unable to work and has been dismissed by his employer. An investigation has revealed that the crash was the result of defective brakes caused by poor maintenance. Can Brian bring a claim against Shuttle Trains plc, the owner of the train? Would it make any difference if Brian had been waiting at the station because he knew his wife would be on that train?

Land Law is the study of the ownership, use of and rights in land and anything fixed to the land. Imagine that you represent Abigail Porter, a middle aged woman who has been living in Surrey with her partner Thomas Swindler for 25 years. The house was purchased in Mr Swindler's sole name, but Abigail was responsible for the refurbishment of the property. She painted all the bedrooms, bought new furniture, and re-tiled the bathroom. She also paid the gas and food bill each month (from her part time job as a classroom assistant in the local school) and was responsible for all the cooking and cleaning. Recently, Thomas has announced that he is leaving Abigail to move in with another woman. He is going to sell the house. Is Abigail entitled to any money from the sale of the house? Would it make any difference if she had contributed to the mortgage, rather than paying the food and gas bills? What if she had also paid for an extension at the back of the house?

Equity and Trusts is the study of the ownership of property on behalf of, and for the benefit of, another. Imagine that you are the judge hearing a case brought by a syndicate of businessmen who have invested in an overseas property portfolio. The businessmen appointed Mr Sly to manage the fund on their behalf. However, Mr Sly was not an honest man and used part of the fund to pay two out of five annual premiums (£10,000 each) on a £1 million life assurance policy for the benefit of his children. He died just after making the fifth payment leaving the children entitled to the £1 million payout. Should the children be entitled to keep the proceeds of the life assurance policy? If not, should they be allowed to keep part of it to reflect the premiums paid by Mr Sly from his own funds? If so, how would you divide the proceeds?

Public Law (Constitutional, Administrative, and Human Rights Law (discussed below)) is the study of the law governing the relationships between state bodies and between legal persons and the state. This broad category would also include Criminal Law and EU Law (discussed above).

Constitutional Law is the study of a system of government and the limits, control and division of government power.

Administrative Law concerns the rights of legal persons to take court action to hold the state to account for its decisions. For example, the process of judicial review allows the legality of decisions made by public bodies to be challenged. Imagine that you act for a couple living in London whose son has been rejected by the local high performing secondary school. The couple tell you that every other child in their street (comprising mainly social housing for low income Eastern European families) has been rejected even though the school is only five minutes away and other children who live further away have been awarded places. Can the families challenge the local authority's admissions policy? What powers do the courts have to investigate such decisions? What action could the families bring?

Human Rights Law concerns particular rights (arising from the European Convention on Human Rights) granted to legal persons to enforce against the state, e.g. the right to a fair trial. Imagine that you represent a client who is subject to a deportation order and is not allowed to see the reasons for this as there is a national security issue at stake. You are not allowed to see the evidence supporting the order and are therefore unable to challenge the evidence or inform your client of the case against him. Can he rely on any human rights arguments to challenge this process?

You will also be expected to engage in legal research as part of your law degree or law conversion course. You will learn how to approach legal problem questions to identify the key legal issues and to advise on the likely outcome of the problem. You will also learn how to approach legal essay questions which tend to focus on contentious areas of law or proposed legal reforms. In doing so, you will learn how to use a law library and electronic databases effectively in order to find sources of law, e.g. case law and legislation. You will also learn how to find, evaluate and analyse academic commentary on particular legal issues.

7 LAW DEGREE V LAW CONVERSION COURSE

As Figure 1 in Ch.5 illustrates, the route to qualification as a solicitor involves two stages of study before you can progress to the training contract. The first is known as the academic stage and consists of a qualifying law degree or a non-qualifying degree (in any subject) plus a law conversion course (the Graduate Diploma in Law (GDL)). The Legal Practice Course (LPC) constitutes the second "vocational" stage.

Some universities offer qualifying combined honours degree programmes. Such programmes satisfy the SRA's requirements in terms of the academic stage of the qualification process while also allowing students to indulge their interest in a non-law subject. Contact individual providers for more information about combined honours programmes.

> We are very open to non-law undergraduates. The skills developed during some degrees, such as English or History, really do provide a good foundation for a legal career.
>
> *Lynn Ford, HR Manager, Blake Lapthorn*

There is no hard evidence to suggest that law firms prefer either law or non-law graduates; firms are generally only interested in getting the best possible graduates. However, it is worth checking with individual firms if you have any concerns about this because some might have particular requirements. The one thing you can rely on is that you will need at least a 2:1 before the City firms (and many of the regional and national firms) will even consider your application and some look as far back as A Levels. While other firms might not have a policy on A Levels and degree classifications, some will weight them against other aspects of their recruitment criteria so you will have to work harder to demonstrate your competence in those areas if you have poor A Levels or a weak degree classification. Firms will also be interested in whether you have studied an academically rigorous degree course and where you studied.

The table below sets out some of the factors to take into account when deciding whether to study law at university or whether to complete a non-qualifying degree and the GDL.

Advantages of a law degree	Advantages of a non-law degree plus GDL
Develop a deeper knowledge of the law	**Intense study of the key legal subjects**
It goes without saying that the depth and breadth of your legal knowledge will be greater if you have studied law for three years at university, rather than one intense year on the GDL. Students on the GDL cover only the core foundation subjects so there is little time to indulge in the finer details of legal research and debate. As a law undergraduate, you will have the opportunity to study specialist options and have more time to find out what areas of law you are actually interested in and thus which practice areas might suit you. You will also have the opportunity to engage in deeper legal research on a specialist topic if you write a dissertation as part of your course.	The GDL is designed to cover the essential foundation subjects in one year while preparing students for the LPC and practice. The teaching therefore tends to be more commercial and practical than is the case on most qualifying law degrees. In reality, you are unlikely to engage in academic debate on the finer points of law during your career as a solicitor, which is why some might argue that the GDL is in fact better preparation for practice than a law degree. Also, since you will have studied all the foundation subjects in one year, they will be more familiar to you when you start your LPC.

Advantages of a law degree	Advantages of a non-law degree plus GDL
Forewarned is forearmed! Early exposure to the realities of legal practice and the study of law might convince you that a legal career is not for you after all, although you will still have a well less respected degree on which to build an alternative career. On the other hand, it could be a very expensive mistake if you only realise this once you have committed to the GDL.	**Last chance to indulge your passion for a particular subject** If you have a burning desire to study a particular non-law subject at university then, provided it is an intellectually challenging, academic degree, you should seriously consider it. You are more likely to excel in a subject that you have a passion for and it will probably be your last chance for academic indulgence for a very long time. It could also be seen as a less risky approach because you are already familiar with that subject, whereas a law degree will be entirely uncharted territory—how do you really know that you will enjoy a law degree if you have not studied it before?

Advantages of a law degree	Advantages of a non-law degree plus GDL
Preparation for interviews/ assessment centres and developing legal skills While it is true that many firms purposely avoid legal content in their recruitment processes, law students sometimes feel more confident about embarking on assessment centres and interviews for training contracts because they are used to "thinking like a lawyer" and have some understanding of core legal principles and current legal issues.	**Breadth of knowledge outside of the law** Non-law graduates can be very strong candidates for training contracts because they bring additional skills and subject knowledge to the work place. This can be especially useful if you want to go into a niche area such as Intellectual Property law where graduates with a science background can be particularly attractive to firms.

Motivation to become a solicitor

If you were to look at most firms' recruitment criteria, one of the key requirements would be for candidates to demonstrate their genuine motivation and commitment to become a solicitor. Firms spend hundreds of thousands of pounds training each trainee so you need to convince prospective employers that you are a serious candidate who is worth the investment. This is especially important in a tough economic climate when firms are more discerning about their choice of trainee and need to differentiate between those who genuinely want to become solicitors and those who are just applying for training contracts because there are fewer jobs in other sectors.

Advantages of a law degree	Advantages of a non-law degree plus GDL
Choosing to study law at university is one way of demonstrating an early commitment to become a solicitor but you should not be complacent; you still need to demonstrate that this was an informed choice and that you have continued to develop your skills during your studies.	Students who embark on the GDL certainly demonstrate motivation to become a solicitor. They have made a conscious decision to study a law conversion course with a view to becoming a solicitor. Firms will be well aware that this is a serious investment in terms of cost, time, and hard work.
Quicker and cheaper By studying a qualifying law degree, you can avoid an extra year of study. This means that your route to qualification will be both quicker and cheaper than your non-law counterparts. Since GDL courses can cost up to nearly £9,000 for a one year full time course starting in 2009 with a London provider, this is a serious advantage for many students. Remember that you will also need to absorb the cost of the LPC (if you are not sponsored), which will increase your fees to somewhere in the region of £20,000.	**Greater life experience** Students who have compled a non-law degree and the GDL have another year of maturity on those who have studied law, which can be appealing to employers.

Advantages of a law degree	Advantages of a non-law degree plus GDL
Earlier careers advice As a law undergraduate, you will probably have greater access to contacts within the legal profession than your non-law counterparts. You will probably also be exposed to tailored careers advice from the first year, which will put you in a stronger position when it comes to early preperation for vacation schemes and training contract applications. It can be more difficult for non-law students to obtain legal careers advice such as how the recruitment process works, how and when to research law firms, when to apply for training contracts, and the importance of getting early work experience, whereas this information tends to be freely available to law undergraduates.	**Very focused careers advice on the GDL** Although you will only have a year in which to build up work experience and work on your training contract applications (if you have not given this any thought while at university), you will have access to high quality, tailored careers advice on the GDL and LPC, particularly where providers specialise solely in legal training. You will also build up a strong network of friends who are focused on the same career goals, which can make for a very stimulating and motivating year of study. In doing so, you will be creating a bank of useful contacts for your long term career.

Advantages of a law degree	Advantages of a non-law degree plus GDL
Well respected by employers	**Keep your options open**
There is no denying the fact that a law degree will be well regarded by employers within the legal sector and elsewhere. A considerable number of law graduates enter alternative employment and training each year, so you would certainly not be limiting your options by choosing to study law at university.	Studying a non-law degree at university gives you more time to choose your career path and experiment with different types of work experience before you commit to a very expensive and rigorous training process.

In some ways it can be more difficult for non-law students to find out about the legal recruitment process. You need to make an extra effort to get work experience and talk to as many people as possible so you go in with your eyes open. However, as long as you have a decent degree, come across well at interview and have obviously made an informed choice to become a lawyer, you should not be at any disadvantage.

Philippa Chatterton, Solicitor, Freshfields

There is one other way of covering the foundations of legal knowledge subjects and that is to take a so-called "senior status degree". These courses are designed for students who already hold a degree in a non-law subject and wish to complete a qualifying law degree in two years, rather than three. They are, however, generally aimed at international students who have completed a degree in their home country and wish to take a "fast track" route through an English law degree.

8 THE LAW DEGREE

A qualifying law degree provides the quickest graduate route to qualification as a solicitor. During your degree, you will gain a thorough understanding of the foundation subjects and explore additional specialist options. You will develop your skills of critical analysis, legal research, and problem solving and should also have the opportunity to participate in extra curricular activities such as mock trials, moots (a mock appeal on a point of law), and negotiation and interviewing competitions.

Applying to Read Law

Universities are ranked according to their performance in a number of different categories. Law firms certainly do look at these league tables and it is fair to say that some still recruit heavily from certain universities. It therefore makes sense to consider the league tables and to apply for the best university your grades will allow. However, you should also engage in some serious (and honest) reflection about what you are hoping to gain from your university experience and consider other factors such as culture, location, quality of teaching and facilities, quality of feedback, career destinations of graduates, whether there is a placement year, extra-curricular activities, accommodation, accessibility of lecturers, research expertise, and pastoral care/student support before making your final decision. The importance attached to each of these factors will vary between individuals and the most important thing is to make the right choice for you.

Essentially, you need to choose a course that you are capable of doing (from academic, financial and practical perspectives), in a location where you will be happy, which will give you a degree that will facilitate your future employment. For example, if you choose a university which is miles from home, you need to make sure you can handle that emotionally. Also, consider the cost of living since this varies enormously throughout the UK. Finally, make an effort to visit the university and reflect on your impression of the campus and staff (both teaching and administrative).

You might want to compare the style of teaching (contact time, teaching hours and methods and the units offered). The facilities are equally important—how impressive is the law library; will you have access to electronic materials; what are the opening hours of the library? The efficacy of the Student Law Society is also important—do they run the events/trips/competitions that you want and need, and how much do they cost? Of course, the last factor is also one of the most important: social life—if you aren't happy at a given university, you won't achieve your full potential, and a decent social life is a key part of that.

Sean Campbell, President of the Student Law Society,
University of Portsmouth

To help you narrow down your choice of institution, your first port of call should be The Guardian University Guide or The Times University Guide. You could also look at the results of the National Student Survey (available at *www.unistats.com*). This is an annual census of final year undergraduates based on the seven areas listed below:

- Quality of Teaching.

- Assessment and Feedback.

- Academic Support.

- Organisation and Management.

- Learning Resources.

- Personal Development.

- Overall Satisfaction.

Once you have narrowed down your choice to a smaller number of universities, it would make sense to visit them to speak with staff and students in person and explore the facilities on offer before making a commitment to spend three or four years at a particular institution. Check individual websites for details of open days and make every effort to attend to get a feel for the city and the culture of the university.

Applications for law degrees are made via UCAS (the University and Colleges Admissions Service). Full details of the application process can be found online at *www.ucas.ac.uk.* Applications for senior status degrees or part time degrees are generally made directly to the relevant institution so you should check individual websites if you are interested in this form of study.

Personal Statements

As with all other UCAS applications, you will be asked to submit a personal statement explaining why you wish to study law. Not all universities interview applicants so the 4,000 characters (including spaces) and 47 lines of the personal statement might well be your only opportunity to convince an Admissions Tutor that you are worth investing in.

Since the personal statement is relatively short, you must construct a convincing and well supported "sales pitch" in a concise, professional and tightly structured style. The statement should explain to the Admissions Tutor why you have chosen to read law at university and why they should make you an offer to join their course. This is a very personal document and should enable the reader to get to know you as an individual. You might find it helpful to consider the following guidance before you start drafting your statement.

Tips for writing a law personal statement

1. Think carefully about structure. Lawyers need to be able to construct persuasive and well structured arguments (supported by evidence) so you should demonstrate these skills in your statement.

2. Think about why you want to study law and consider the best way to convey your interest, commitment and enthusiasm to the Admissions Tutor. Perhaps you are interested in a particular area of law, or perhaps you have been inspired by a period of work experience or an event in your own life, or perhaps by a book you have read, or an event or issue that you have been following in the news. Some students include quotations as a hook to capture the interest of the reader. This can be very effective but you must choose an appropriate quotation and it should complement the rest of your statement, rather than appearing as though you have thrown it in without really thinking about it or understanding its significance.

3. Think about what makes a good law student. How can you demonstrate that you fit this profile? Could you draw on the skills you have developed during your A Level studies, or through positions of responsibility that you held at school or sixth form, or from your work experience?

4. What are your future career plans? How does the law degree fit into those plans? Do you have any relevant work experience that you could discuss? This should not be a major part of the statement, but would be worth mentioning.

5. Think about what you will bring to the university. Draw on your extra-curricular activities and achievements to support your claims.

6. Ideally, you should use your personal statement to address any gaps in your academic history and show what you have learnt from your experiences.

7. It is up to you whether you use your personal statement to address any extenuating circumstances, or whether you ask your tutors to raise such matters in the academic reference. If you are not sure how to approach particular difficulties, discuss your concerns with your parents, tutors and/or careers advisor.

8. Admissions Tutors have very little time to read these statements (perhaps only a minute or two for each one). Therefore, you should avoid superfluous words and flowery language and instead adopt a concise, direct style with short sentences.

9. Proof read your work. Lawyers are expected to pay attention to detail!

10. Show the draft to parents and tutors to comment on. They know you better than anyone and will be an invaluable source of guidance when it comes to writing the personal statement.

Do GCSEs and A Levels Matter?

Students at school or sixth form often ask whether they should study particular subjects at GCSE and A Level if they want to read Law at university. For GCSEs or the International Baccalaureate you have slightly more flexibility because of the number of subjects covered, although you are advised to focus predominantly on traditional academic subjects rather than too many practical, arts based, or vocational subjects.

In terms of A Levels, it is worth checking with individual universities as they do vary and some have particularly strong preferences. It is also worth considering your academic profile from the perspective of future employers. While a particular qualification might secure entry to a university course, consider how attractive is it likely to be to a law firm that has the pick of the very best graduates. Aside from university specific requirements, the best advice would be to stick to traditional academic subjects but choose those that you enjoy and in which you are likely to do well. There is some merit in taking at least one of the humanities subjects as this will be good preparation for the type of research, reading, analysis and essay writing that you will have to engage with during a law degree. However, science subjects can be useful preparation for some specialist areas of law such as intellectual property and they also help develop logical thought processes and problem solving skills, which are useful when it comes to approaching legal case studies.

Another common question is whether there is any advantage, or indeed disadvantage, to studying A Level Law before embarking on a Law degree. There are mixed views on this issue and it is worth checking with the Admissions Tutors at individual universities to find out what position they have adopted. Some students say that they were pleased that they studied Law at A Level because it meant that some of the concepts in the first year of university were familiar to them, others suggest that since law is taught differently at university compared to A Level it is easier to begin with a "clean slate".

> Some of my friends had studied A Level Law and I think this probably did help them a bit in the first year because some of the topics were familiar to them, but they didn't always get to grips with it at degree level. I think you just need to be aware that this is a higher level of study; you won't do well if you think you know it all already.
>
> *A Law Undergraduate*

The one thing about which there can be no doubt is that A Level grades matter. It is becoming increasingly common for law firms to take them into account as part of the recruitment process and some of the City firms will not consider applicants with lower than 340/320 UCAS points, i.e. AAB/ABB at A Level (or equivalent qualifications). Make no mistake about it, competition in the legal recruitment process is fierce and A Levels are the first hurdle to be crossed. Even if firms do not specify minimum A Level requirements, they will be taken into account at some stage and might be all that differentiates you from another equally strong candidate. Therefore, whatever grades your chosen university requires, it makes sense to work as hard as you can to achieve the best possible marks so that you keep your options open when it comes to applying for training contracts.

The National Admissions Test for Law (LNAT)

The LNAT (England's equivalent of the American Law School Admissions Test (LSAT)) is an independent national aptitude test for law. It was launched in 2004 and adopted by eight institutions as a response to the increasing difficulties faced by universities when forced to differentiate between candidates with similarly high A Level results. It is now required by 10 institutions for 2010 entry (or 2011 deferred entry) for both home and international applicants.

The LNAT is an online test, which includes a mixture of multiple choice questions and an essay question designed to test your powers of critical thinking and reasoning. It is an aptitude test so it is not possible to "revise" particular topics but, since there is no opportunity to re-sit the test in any single application cycle, is it advisable to have some practice runs before you visit the test centre so you know what to expect.

Practical issues

Your LNAT result consists of the mark out of 30 for the multiple choice section of the test. Your response to the essay question is stored on-line for Admissions Tutors to access and review if they wish. You will be notified by email of your LNAT result and your chosen universities will also be notified automatically. Note, however, that the results are only available to those institutions that use the test as part of their application procedure. This means that if you apply to any other universities (i.e.

ones that do not require the LNAT), they will not see the results of your test.

You can sit the test at one of over a hundred test centres throughout the country but you must register, book and pay for the test in advance via the LNAT website. The current fee for candidates at UK test centres is approximately £40 (this is payable on-line when you book the test). If you are worried about the cost of this test, you should check the LNAT website for details of the LNAT Bursary Scheme. Support is also available for those claiming state benefits.

It is your responsibility to arrange and sit the LNAT. Universities will not be sympathetic to those who, for whatever reason, claim that they have not been able to do so. Be proactive and do not rely on your school or sixth form to make the arrangements. Registration opens in the August of the year in which you intend to submit your UCAS application and testing begins in September. If you are applying to an institution that requires the LNAT, you should visit the LNAT website early and make a note of the key deadlines for completing the test (these vary between universities).

It is also your responsibility to notify the test administrators if you need extra time to complete the test, or have special access requirements, as a result of a disability. Check the LNAT website for details of how to do this and make sure that you get it organised as early as possible.

Tips for the LNAT

1. The LNAT website (*www.lnat.ac.uk*) has some useful hints and tips on how to prepare for the test.

2. The LNAT website has some sample questions and there are various books on the market which contain practice multiple choice questions, sample essay questions, and tips for success. See the Further Reading appendix for some suggested texts.

3. You will not lose marks for an incorrect answer so you should try to answer all the questions in the multiple choice section.

4. Try to get into the habit of reading a quality newspaper every day. This will ensure that you are up to speed with current affairs and will add substance to your response to the essay question. It will also

help you to think about how to construct a persuasive argument when constrained by a limited word count (you will have 40 minutes and a maximum of 750 words in which to write your response). Do not just read the newspapers passively though; the LNAT tests your skills of critical thinking and analysis and your ability to build a persuasive argument so it would make sense to try to develop these skills through your reading. Think about what assumptions are made in the article. How persuasive are the points made by the writer? What would the counter arguments be? How effective is the structure of the article? Is it likely that the writer is giving a balanced view of the issue? Do you think the writer is influenced by a particular perspective (political or otherwise)?

5. Try to get a good night's sleep the night before the test; give yourself plenty of time to get to the test centre; follow all the instructions in the paper; read each question slowly and carefully; and keep an eye on the clock during the test to ensure that you have time to answer all the questions.

The Successful Law Student

Whatever anyone tells you, and whatever method(s) your university uses to calculate its final degree classifications, do not make the mistake of believing that your first year grades are not important. Law undergraduates can begin applying for training contracts in their second year of study, and all students should build up their body of work experience during their first and second year at university to support future training contract applications. Think about what you are going to be putting on those application forms and/or speculative letters requesting work experience: A Level results and first year university grades. This is the only information prospective employers will have about your academic profile. Do not fall down at the first hurdle because your first year grades are poor.

Module choices are important. Firms will question you about your undergraduate modules, so make sure you can explain why you did them and how they fit into the bigger picture, your career. Don't think that your first and second year marks are unimportant. You should be applying for

training contracts while you are an undergraduate and applications will ask you for all of your module marks.
Danielle Spalding, LPC student, Bristol Institute of Legal Practice.

What is it like to study at university?

Students are often concerned about how university differs from school or sixth form. The main difference is the emphasis on "independent learning". This means that you are responsible for your own learning; the tutors will simply direct you to relevant materials and provide an outline structure for that learning.

Teaching for each unit will normally be divided into lectures and seminars. Lectures consist of large groups of students (possibly as many as 200) with one lecturer. Lectures introduce key topics by setting out the basic principles and highlighting any controversial issues or law reform proposals. They also direct students to important cases or articles for further reading. There will be little, if any, student interaction. Your role will be to listen actively to the lecturer and make effective notes to support your own independent study of the topic. The lecture is not intended to tell you everything you need to know about a particular topic (hence the focus on independent learning); you will need to build up your knowledge by preparing for, and participating in, seminars and reading around the subject.

Seminars are much smaller groups of students with a seminar leader (either a tutor or sometimes a research student). These classes provide an opportunity to explore particular issues in more depth than is possible in a lecture. Seminars very often focus on topics that are likely to be assessed in the exam or coursework, and they offer students the opportunity to discuss any concerns or raise any questions related to particular topics. Attendance is therefore crucial, but attendance alone is not enough: you must also engage fully with the preparatory reading, and contribute in class. Seminars should not turn into "mini lectures"; this is frustrating for the tutor and a poor learning experience for the students.

The accreditation requirements of the Solicitors Regulation Authority mean that the foundation subjects are assessed largely by way of exam although some institutions might introduce a coursework component (perhaps 20 per cent to 30 per cent of the final grade). Exams usually consist of a mixture of essay and problem questions. A problem question is a fictional scenario (similar to those given in Ch.6) in which you are asked to identify and apply the relevant law in order to reach a conclusion as to the likely outcome of the particular situation. An essay question will focus on the critical analysis of a particular area of law or topical legal issue. There is more flexibility with other non-core units, which might be assessed by way of exam, coursework, group or individual presentation, extended research project, or a moot (a mock appeal on a particular point of law).

What makes a good law student?

There is no such thing as a model student, but successful law students certainly share some common characteristics. Most of those characteristics can be developed with hard work and commitment so there is no reason why you should not become a member of this group.

One of the most important keys to success is to keep an open mind and to try to be positive and enthusiastic about your studies. This might sound obvious but it is something that many students fail to do. You are bound to find some elements of the law degree dry and rather complicated. However, try not to dwell on those areas and instead focus on the aspects of the course that you find interesting. Students who adopt a positive attitude and maintain enthusiasm and passion for their subject will probably get better results and will certainly get more satisfaction from their studies.

You will also do better, and enjoy your studies more, if you have a deep understanding of your subject, rather than just skimming the surface. Deep understanding is achieved by really getting to grips with the detail of a particular area of law, understanding how it is applied to practical situations, and subjecting it to critical analysis. This cannot be achieved by relying solely on your lecture notes; it can only be achieved by wider reading and independent study. By all means start with your lecture notes and a basic textbook to gain an understanding of the key principles, but also dip into academic articles, judgments from key cases, and monographs (a work that focuses on a single subject very often arising from a PhD thesis). Academic articles can be particularly useful in terms of identifying parallels with other areas of law; comparing the approach taken under English law with the approaches adopted in other jurisdictions; and considering how academics have responded to particular judgments or new pieces of legislation. Reading academic articles will also show you how to critically analyse a legal principle or judgment, rather than just describing it as your textbooks will tend to do. Many textbooks contain further reading lists at the end of each chapter and your tutor will also be able to recommend additional texts and articles.

As a law student, you should be prepared for hard work and long hours in the library and you will need to manage your time wisely. Keep a note of key assessment deadlines and make sure that you give yourself plenty of time to get the work done. You might well find that a number of deadlines fall at a similar time, but tutors will not be sympathetic if you express difficulty in meeting them. Remember that the focus is on independent learning so it is your responsibility to manage your time and achieve all that is asked of you within a particular period.

Organisation and self motivation are the keys to a successful degree. You must know what you need to do, and when you need to do it, and then find the motivation to get on and do it . . . you will find that you have an immense amount of free time in some periods and an equally immense workload during others. It is effective organisation that allows you to balance this out.

> Sean Campbell, President of the Student Law Society,
> University of Portsmouth

There will be a considerable amount of reading and seminar preparation to get through and the trick is to be selective about what you read. You do not have to read every case, but it would be worth reading the judgments of key cases so that you can see why the judges reached a particular decision and whether there were any dissenting judgments (those that disagreed with the ultimate decision). If you get used to reading cases and academic articles from your first year, you will find it less daunting when you come to engage in research for your dissertation.

In my first year, I don't think I read many full cases but in my second year I read more of the judgments and I've found that has really helped in understanding the key principles, why decisions were made in particular cases and what points the judges disagreed on. Having said that, I don't think you physically have the time to read every single case, especially if you are getting involved in other activities and building up your CV at the same time.

A Law Undergraduate

Another factor related to effective time management is an ability to make good notes. This does not mean reading a textbook and copying out chunks of text, nor writing down every word a lecturer says (even if you could write that quickly). It means thinking about what you are reading or listening to, and being selective about what you write down and how you present it. Note making should be an organic process, which means you should treat your notes as "work in progress" to be revisited and supplemented after each seminar and in light of your wider reading. Keep your notes organised and consolidate each topic as you work through the course.

Lastly, make sure that you are engaged in active, rather than passive, learning. Active learning can mean lots of things, including participating in class discussions, working in a study group sharing information and knowledge, or practising past exam questions. It does not mean sitting for hours in the library in front of the same textbook reading the same passage over again. Neither does it mean copying out reams of notes from textbooks or judgments and then filing them away until the exams. A full file of beautifully written notes might look impressive, but it will be of little comfort if you do not actually understand any of the content, let alone how to apply it to exam questions.

At the end of each topic, have a go at some past exam papers to see how well you actually understand the topic. The more practice papers you complete, the more you will develop your technique so it should become second nature by the time you reach the final exams. Do not leave everything until just before the exams: you will not obtain the best marks if you rely on revision guides and last minute cramming.

Preparation and organisation are fundamental to successfully completing a law degree. Treat it like a nine to five job (you can still have a life at night and at weekends). Plan your time effectively, know when your deadlines are and give yourself enough time to complete assessments without rushing. It is also important to get feedback from assessments and try to use it constructively to improve your next assignment. Lastly, use your lecturers and seminar tutors. Most are happy to answer queries

if you have any concerns and some will mark practice exam answers in
the build up to assessment periods.
Tom Storey, Third Year Law Undergraduate, University of Portsmouth

Tips for success

1. Make sure you attend, and prepare for, all lectures and seminars
   and participate actively during group discussions.

2. Find the library early on and make use of it. Also get to know the
   law librarian in your first year. He will be an invaluable source of
   knowledge as you progress through the degree, especially if you
   have to write a dissertation in your final year.

3. Read widely and try to move beyond recommended reading
   lists.

4. Engage in active learning.

5. Consolidate your notes at the end of each topic and learn the key
   cases as you go along; do not ignore them until just before the
   exams.

6. Draw on support from your peers by forming study groups (but
   make sure you choose like-minded students who share your goals
   and aspirations).

7. Get copies of past exam papers at the beginning of each unit to
   familiarise yourself with the format of the exams and identify any
   topics that seem to crop up each year.

8. Make sure you practise problem questions and essay questions.
   There is a technique to this and you will not get the best grades in
   exams if you fail to master it.

9. Keep an open mind and try to develop a positive and enthusiastic
   approach to your studies.

10. Make time to relax with friends and get involved in extra-
    curricular activities. This will ensure that you do not burn yourself
    out and will also help to enhance and develop your CV.

It is a challenging course and it does take time to get to grips with the work but if you get too bogged down in the work and it stresses you out then you won't be able to get involved in all the extra curricular and social activities on offer and these are important if you want to become a solicitor. You need to know that you can manage your time effectively and understand that different times of the year bring varying demands on your time.

Jo Pennick, Third Year Law Undergraduate, King's College London

Nicholas McBride gives some very helpful tips on how to become an effective law student in his book called Letters to a Law Student. You can also find some excellent guidance in Sheila Cottrell's book, The Study Skills Handbook.

9 THE GRADUATE DIPLOMA IN LAW: CONVERTING TO LAW

Students without a qualifying law degree must complete a law conversion course before progressing to the vocational stage of training (the LPC). The Graduate Diploma in Law (GDL) provides an introduction to the English Legal System and legal research skills, and covers the seven foundations of legal knowledge. The GDL is offered at over 40 providers throughout England and Wales (some of which have campuses in a number of different cities) and can be completed on a full time basis over one year or part time over two years.

You might sometimes see the term CPE (Common Professional Exam) used interchangeably with the term GDL. This course was the previous incarnation of the GDL although it is effectively the same qualification. Some practitioners and the Solicitors Regulation Authority continue to use this term, although course providers tend to use the term GDL or the more colloquial "law conversion course".

You really need to give serious thought as to whether or not a legal career is for you before you embark on the GDL. It is a very expensive and labour intensive course and there are arguably far better ways to spend your time and money if you do not want to be a solicitor.

What really strikes me when I think about the GDL is how many people were taking the course at such great cost to themselves and how many of them have still not got training contracts or who didn't even go onto complete the LPC. You have to know that you are going to want it. It's a lot of money and it might not necessarily suit you so really think hard before you embark on the course.

A GDL Graduate

Assessment

You will need to research individual providers to find out whether their courses are assessed wholly by exam, or whether they include any coursework components. It would also be worth finding out how long the

exam period lasts, and whether there is a revision week or reading week
built into the course.

Each assessment can be repeated a maximum of three times. If a
student fails any exam more than three times, they must re-take the whole
course or complete a law degree. The pass mark for the GDL is 40 per
cent and your overall performance on the course will be graded as
'Distinction', 'Commendation', or 'Pass'.

> The format of GDL assessments will vary between providers but most
> contain a mix of essay-type questions and problem scenarios where you
> will be required to apply the legal principles you have learned to a new
> set of facts. The questions are usually reflective of the sorts of problems
> you will encounter during seminars and a good course will allow you lots
> of opportunity to practise answering questions like this. Some GDL
> providers also include an element of assessed coursework.
>
> *Kerry James, Course Director of the Legal Practice Course,*
> *Bristol Institute of Legal Practice*

Choosing Your Provider

You should research conversion course providers carefully to ensure that
you make the right choice for you in terms of location, culture, cost,
course structure, class sizes, opportunities for flexible study, and methods
of teaching and assessment.

You might like to consider the following factors when choosing your
provider:

1. **Course fees**—the GDL can cost up to £9,000 for a full time course
   with a London provider starting in 2009 (although some providers
   charge much less than this) so cost is likely to be a key
   consideration. Do not allow this to be your only concern though;
   you must also make sure that you are happy with the quality of the
   course and the level of support provided to students. Most firms do
   not mind where you study as long as the foundation subjects are
   covered. However, it is worth bearing in mind that the GDL is a
   very intense course, particularly if you are also searching for a
   training contract during that year, so you should ensure that you

will have access to good quality teaching, a good support network and facilities, and an excellent careers service.

2. **Student numbers and class sizes**—these can vary enormously between providers and will obviously affect the culture and atmosphere of a particular course.

3. **Teaching methods and facilities**—find out how the course is delivered and how much face-to-face teaching you will have. You might wish to find out about part time study opportunities and, if you are planning to commute from home, how often you will actually need to be on campus. Find out about the level of pastoral care and the standard of teaching and IT facilities. You should also look at the quality of the library, careers facilities and other student support services. Where a provider offers the GDL and a law degree, you might also be interested in whether the GDL students are mixed in with the undergraduates or whether they are taught separately

4. **Extra-curricular activities**—it is important to continue to build up your CV during your GDL year so consider how the provider supports students in doing so. Are there Pro Bono opportunities? Does the provider participate in client interviewing and negotiation competitions? What support is there for students who wish to enter such competitions? Are there student societies and sports teams?

5. **Teaching materials**—find out what materials are provided (e.g. textbooks, statute books, case books and lecture handbooks) and what you will be expected to buy. Also try to find out about the quality of lecture notes, revision notes, seminar packs, and other teaching materials.

6. **Quality of careers support**—this is especially important if you have not already secured a training contract. Does the provider have a law fair? If so, who attends? Find out about the provider's links with the legal profession. Do they operate a mentoring scheme to put students in touch with practitioners?

7. **Location**—courses vary considerably in terms of cost, and location can have a bearing on this (with London courses and the

associated living costs being an extremely expensive option). If you are a self-funding student, you might like to consider providers close to home so that you can save money. The GDL is an intense year and some students are glad to take advantage of support at home. Also think about where you want to practise as many providers have close links with the local legal community. It will also make it easier to take time out for interviews and open days if you are studying in the area.

8. **Additional qualifications**—some providers give non-law graduates the opportunity to 'top up' to an LLB award (law degree) if they have completed both the GDL and LPC with them. Contact individual providers directly if this is something that might be of interest to you.

9. **The structure of the course**—most providers run all GDL modules right across the year with all assessments held at the end, during the summer term. Some providers split the course so that students take four subjects in the first half of the academic year, which are assessed in the early spring, and the rest in the second half of the year, which are assessed in the summer. This may be a more manageable structure, given the heavy workload, and is certainly worth considering when choosing your provider.

As part of your research, you should visit providers' websites and make an effort to attend open days to get a feel for the culture of the institution and find out more about the surrounding area. You should also speak to representatives and current students at law fairs, and consult tutors or careers advisors for advice. You might also find the profiles at *www .targetcourses.co.uk/home* helpful.

Applying for the GDL

Applications for law conversion courses are made via the Central Applications Board (*www.lawcabs.ac.uk*). You can download a sample application form from the Central Applications Board website. You can apply to up to three institutions and will be asked to list them in order of preference. You will also be asked to pay a £10 non-refundable application fee to and to arrange for a tutor to provide an academic reference by email.

The initial round of applications opens in early November and ends in mid-April. To be considered in the first round, your application form, application fee, and reference must be received by February 1. Applications received after February 1, but before the end of the initial stage, will be considered at the beginning of April. Applications received after the end of the initial stage may still be considered subject to the continued availability of places.

Visit the website for more details of the application process and to check key deadlines. For part time, or distance learning courses, applications should be made directly to the relevant provider.

Tips for Success on the GDL

When you choose to study the GDL, you make a commitment to becoming a professional lawyer, either a solicitor or a barrister. Try to think of yourself not so much as a student, but as someone embarking on their professional training. You are not on the course to skip classes or to get away with minimal effort: you are there to learn as much as you can to help you when you get into practice. Treat it as a job and try to work office hours. This mindset will ease you through both the GDL and the LPC and you will hit the ground running when you begin your training contract.

Kerry James, Course Director of the Legal Practice Course,
Bristol Institute of Legal Practice

The GDL is an intense year and should be taken seriously from the outset. In reality, you will be cramming the best part of a three year law degree into a one year course. There is a lot of ground to cover, an astonishing amount of reading, and new skills of analysis and problem solving to be developed. You should expect to feel overwhelmed at some point during the course, but you will not be alone and must try to remember that it is just a year and a vital stepping stone to your future career.

The difficulty with the GDL is that it moves incredibly fast so, if you get behind, it is very easy to come unstuck—there just aren't enough hours in the day to catch up if you fall behind because the topics are so tightly packed.

Thomas Moore, Solicitor, Gregory Rowcliffe Milners

1. Keep on top of the work from the very first day. The course moves at an incredibly fast pace so you cannot afford to get behind. Treat the course like a professional job and make time each day to consolidate what you have learnt and prepare for your next class.

Treat the GDL like a treadmill—you just have to keep going. It's only a year so just immerse yourself in it and keep on top of the work. I worked a 9–5 day (maybe not even that) and that worked. That way, all your tutorial notes are up to date, you've studied every case, and when it comes to revision it's not actually that hard. If you try to cram it all in at the end, there's just too much information to cope with. We had to learn something like 700 cases and you just can't get that into last minute revision sessions.

Jonathan Pugh-Smith, Trainee Solicitor, Berwin Leighton Paisner LLP

2. Keep your notes in order as you go along. Do not leave it all until the revision period, there simply will not be time.

My GDL involved eight exams in two weeks, which was quite tough, but I'm the kind of person who does their homework so I just worked all the way through and kept on top of it. If you keep on top of it throughout the year then you're halfway there when it comes to revision."

A GDL Graduate

3. Attend every lecture and seminar. Do not be tempted to skip a class and catch up on the reading later. The classes are an essential part of the course and will direct you to the most important aspects of a particular topic for the purposes of the assessment. A good GDL course will distil the mass of information arising from each foundation subject into manageable chunks, and the teaching materials and seminars will be closely focused towards the assessment. If you do not take advantage of this guidance, you will probably find the volume of work unmanageable and there is a real risk that you could fail your assessments.

4. Consider forming a study group. You could divide up the reading for each seminar and share your knowledge with the rest of the group, or perhaps you could share lecture notes or swap

essay plans for practice exam papers. The students on a GDL course tend to be focused and professional in the way they approach their studies because they are making a serious investment in their chosen career path. You will find therefore that most people are motivated to do well and happy to pull their weight in group work.

5. Be selective about what you learn and what you read. Although you are covering the same foundation subjects, this is not a law degree and therefore you cannot be expected to cover everything in the same level of detail as a law undergraduate. By all means read the judgments of key cases in full, but for other cases it is fine to rely on a case book or even a good textbook.

6. Find out about the format of the exams as early as possible and get through as many practice papers as you can during the year. Given the limited time available, your learning must be targeted and practice exam papers will help you to get the focus right. They also reduce the risk of a nasty shock when it comes to the assessment period.

7. Make a note of key deadlines and manage your time. You should be putting in a full working week and working consistently throughout the whole year, rather than leaving it all until the last minute. Stick to a strict study plan but also make time for extra-curricular activities and socialising. This is a very tough year but you do need some light relief to avoid burning yourself out.

8. Make good use of your holidays for work experience and careers based activities. You cannot afford to lose sight of the ultimate goal: securing a training contract. If you find it difficult to fit things in during term-time, you will have to make effective use of your holidays. The year will pass quickly: before you know it you will be embarking on the LPC and time will be running out to secure a training contract.

9. Use the Easter holidays to get a head start on revision. Although some providers incorporate a revision period into the course programme, this is unlikely to give you sufficient time to prepare fully for the exams.

Do not forget about your long term career goal

One of the main challenges of the GDL is the combination of intense academic study with the search for a training contract. Competition is fierce and, having invested considerable time and money in the conversion course, you cannot afford to lose your focus when it comes to building up your CV and making applications for training contracts. Even if you do not apply for training contracts during your GDL year, you should continue to develop your experience so that you have plenty to draw on when it comes to making applications during your LPC.

Take advantage of your careers service and, however busy you are, make a concerted effort to attend any careers events such as law fairs, guest lectures or workshops. Also take advantage of any existing contacts and try to arrange as much work experience as possible during the holidays. If you can manage it alongside your studies, try to build in some time to join pro bono projects or participate in negotiation or interviewing competitions.

10 THE LEGAL PRACTICE COURSE (LPC)

The LPC was quite a relief because I had found my law degree difficult. It was really refreshing to do the LPC where suddenly the focus is so much more practical and based on what you will actually do as a trainee. It was a good preparation for practice.

A Trainee Solicitor

Completion of the LPC is a compulsory requirement in order to qualify as a solicitor; it is known as the vocational stage of training. Students must have completed the academic stage of training before enrolling on the LPC although some courses, known as 'Exempting Law Degrees', combine both the academic stage and the LPC.

The LPC provides the transition between the academic stage of the qualification process and your training contract. During the LPC you learn how to apply legal principles in a practical setting. For example, on the law degree or GDL you learn the principles of Land Law as an academic subject, but on the LPC you learn the how to sell or lease a property. Similarly, during the academic stage of training you learn the principles of Contract Law, but on the LPC you learn how to bring a contractual dispute to court.

The tasks you carry out during the LPC look very much like the tasks that would be asked of a trainee solicitor. There is a significant emphasis on learning the skills you need for practice, so that you "learn by doing". You will role play client interviews, make applications to court, draft letters of advice and formal legal documents, and research practical problems using practitioner resources. Because of this practical emphasis, much of the LPC is not as difficult conceptually as the degree or the GDL but the workload is heavy and some students find it difficult to switch into a true understanding of what is needed from a client's perspective.

The Structure of the LPC

While certain core units must be covered, recent changes approved by the Solicitors Regulation Authority have given considerable autonomy to

LPC providers in terms of the design and focus of their courses. This has enabled providers to tailor courses to particular types of firm or practice areas and to place greater emphasis on particular units or skills. It has also provided greater flexibility for students.

Traditionally, the LPC was completed either as a one year full time course or a two year part time course. However, changes approved by the Solicitors Regulation Authority in 2008 (to be fully implemented by September 2010) mean that it is now possible to take advantage of the "new style" LPC which provides greater flexibility for students in terms of the time taken to complete their studies and the choice of institutions and electives. The new LPC is divided into two stages:

Stage 1—this stage covers the core practice areas and skills units.

Stage 2—this stage consists of three vocational electives.

Providers can be authorised to provide either of Stages 1 or 2, or both of them. Students must complete Stage 1 with a single provider, but Stage 2 can be completed with three separate providers if the student chooses to do so. Both Stages 1 and 2 must be completed and passed within a five year period (running from the date on which the student attempts the first assessment) regardless of whether they are full or part time students. If there is an outstanding Stage 2 subject after the expiry of this period, the student must repeat both Stage 1 and Stage 2 in their entirety and pass all assessments.

The increased window of five years within which to complete the LPC course is likely to be particularly attractive to those who wish to spread the cost of their studies over a longer period, or those who choose to combine their studies with work. Indeed, it is now possible for students to start their training contract while studying for the LPC provided that Stage 1 is completed and passed before the Professional Skills Course (PSC) is taken (see Ch.11 for further details on the PSC). The fact that students can complete Stage 2 at three different providers also means that they can tailor their vocational electives to the work of a particular firm or type of firm if one provider does not offer all the specialist options that they are interested in.

For more details on the new LPC, visit the Solicitors Regulation Authority website (*www.sra.org.uk/students/lpc/lpc-update.page*).

The LPC felt quite evenly paced compared to the GDL. Certainly it is conceptually less challenging, although the volume of work remains high.

Thomas Moore, Solicitor, Gregory Rowcliffe Milners

Stage 1

Subject	What will you do?
Professional Conduct and Regulation	Learn about professional ethics and the importance of client care. This will include understanding the relevance of financial services and money laundering regulation to solicitors and their work, and also the distinction between office and client money and the rules and procedures governing the collection, investment, accounting and use of each one.
Wills and Administration of Estates	Learn about the administration of an estate when someone dies testate (leaving a will) and intestate (without a will).
Taxation	Learn about different methods of taxation and tax planning.

Core Skills

Core Skill	What will you do?
Practical Legal Research	Learn how to approach legal problem questions to identify the key legal issue and how to report your findings to your client(s). Develop research skills to enable you to engage effectively and efficiently in legal research using a law library and electronic databases.

Core Skill	What will you do?
Writing and Drafting	Prepare professional correspondence such as letters, reports and memoranda and learn how to draft legal documentation.
Interviewing and Advising	Learn how to conduct a client interview in order to find out more about the client's situation and desired outcome. Learn how to gather the relevant facts and identify irrelevant information. Present advice in a manner that is appropriate to the particular client, which will often involve explaining complex legal issues in an accessible and meaningful manner.
Advocacy	Learn how to present your case effectively in court and how to argue points of law from a particular perspective.

The Core Practice Areas

Practice Area	What will you do?
Business Law and Practice	Learn about the different vehicles available to individuals who wish to start their own businesses, e.g. sole trader, partnership, limited company, etc. Learn about the legal issues arising from various business relationships and what happens when businesses get into financial difficulties. Learn about the methods of taxation that affect companies and those involved in their management and/or ownership.

Practice Area	What will you do?
Property Law and Practice	Learn about the practical, legal and regulatory issues surrounding the sale and purchase of property, and the procedure to be followed by solicitors in order to acquire or dispose of property on behalf of their clients.
Litigation	Learn how civil cases are conducted in the High Court and County Court. Also learn how criminal cases are conducted, including powers of arrest and the procedures to be followed at the police station.

Stage 2

Vocational Electives

Different providers offer different options so it is important to do your research to choose the course that best suits your areas of interest and aspirations for practice. Vocational electives cover a wide range of legal practice areas enabling you to maintain a broad knowledge base, or to specialise in a particular area. Options include:

- immigration and asylum;
- children (public law);
- family and children (private law);
- charity law;
- housing;
- social welfare law;
- planning and environmental law;
- intellectual property;
- media and entertainment;

- IT law;
- advanced civil litigation and advocacy;
- corporate finance (equity);
- commercial property;
- commercial law;
- banking and capital markets;
- advanced criminal litigation and advocacy;
- employment;
- commercial dispute resolution;
- acquisitions and mergers; and
- public sector organisations.

Methods of Assessment

The Solicitors Regulation Authority states that assessment of the core practice units and the vocational elective units must be by way of a three hour (minimum) exam or other supervised assessment.

Professional conduct and regulation must be assessed partly by way of a discrete two hour (minimum) assessment and partly by allocating 5 per cent of the marks in each core practice assessment to professional conduct/regulatory issues. There will also be a separate two hour (minimum) supervised assessment of the Solicitors Accounts Rules.

Like the GDL, each assessment can be repeated a maximum of three times. If a student fails any Stage 1 assessment on the third attempt, they will fail the whole of Stage 1. If a student fails any vocational elective unit on the third attempt, they will have to re-enrol on that elective course, or enrol on a different elective course. The pass mark for all core and elective assessments is 50 per cent. The skills assessments are graded as either competent or not yet competent.

Choosing a Provider

The LPC is offered by around 30 providers throughout England and Wales (some of which have campuses in a number of different cities).

Some firms specify particular LPC providers for their trainees and some even commission tailor made courses where their solicitors are involved in the preparation and delivery of some of the teaching materials.

We had a 'tailor made' LPC which meant that we studied our core compulsory subjects with people going to different firms but our electives were BLP specific. This involved using the firm's precedents and attending talks given by BLP partners and interactive workshops run by other fee earners relating to their particular area of work.

Clare Reeve, Trainee Solicitor, Berwin Leighton Paisner LLP

It is worth looking at different LPC providers as they vary in terms of course content, culture, teaching methods, and the level of course fees. Unless firms specify particular providers, they are more likely to be concerned about what options you chose to study rather than where you completed the course. For example, a student who has studied public sector organisations, social welfare law and advanced criminal litigation and advocacy is likely to be less appealing to a national commercial firm or a City firm than someone who studied banking and capital markets, commercial law, and commercial property.

Choose the provider that will work best for you and suit your learning preferences. The way my provider structured the LPC probably wouldn't be right for everyone—I was only in college for about two and a half hours four days a week to begin with so I had to do everything else myself. That's not going to work for everyone: some people might prefer a provider with more structure and classroom time.

A Trainee Solicitor

You might like to consider some of these factors when choosing your provider:

1. **Course fees**—the LPC can cost up to £12,500 for a full time course with a London provider starting in 2009 (although some providers charge less than this). Some of the larger commercial firms will sponsor their trainees through the LPC by paying course fees and perhaps also providing a maintenance grant. However, if you are self-funding, the level of fees is likely to be an important factor in your choice of provider. Do not allow this to be your only

concern though: you must also make sure that you are happy with the quality of the course and the level of support provided to students.

2. **Student numbers and class sizes**—these can vary considerably between providers and will obviously affect the culture and atmosphere of a particular course.

3. **Choice of vocational electives**—this is likely to be particularly important to you if you wish to specialise in a niche area of legal practice, or if you intend to target particular firms when you apply for training contracts. However, beware of limiting your options too much if you have not secured a training contract by the time you start the course.

4. **Teaching methods and facilities**—find out how the course is delivered and how much face-to-face teaching you will have. You might wish to find out about part time study opportunities and, if you are planning to commute from home, how often you will actually need to be on campus. Find out about the level of pastoral care and the standard of teaching and IT facilities. You should also look at the quality of the library, careers facilities and other student support services—these are likely to be very important to you when you start the course.

5. **Teaching materials**—find out what materials are provided (e.g. textbooks, statute books, case books and lecture handbooks) and what you will be expected to buy. Also try to find out about the quality of lecture notes, revision notes, seminar packs, and other teaching materials.

6. **Extra-curricular activities**—it is important to continue to build up your CV during your LPC year so it makes sense to consider how the provider supports students in doing so. Are there Pro Bono opportunities? Does the provider participate in client interviewing and negotiation competitions? What support is there for students who wish to enter such competitions? Are there student societies and sports teams?

7. **Quality of careers support**—this is especially important if you have not secured a training contract by the time you leave

university or complete the GDL. By committing to the LPC without a training contract, you are making a serious financial investment and you should be looking for reassurance that your provider will provide targeted support for those still searching for a training contract. Does the provider have a law fair? If so, who attends? What percentage of students start the course without a training contract and how many have secured one by the time they leave? Find out about the provider's links with the legal profession. Do they operate a mentoring scheme to put students in touch with practitioners?

> So many people failed to take advantage of the careers support available at my LPC provider, which was such a waste. I found them really helpful: they looked at my CV and gave me a mock interview; it all really helped.
>
> *A College of Law LPC Graduate*

8. **Location**—there will be time for enjoying yourself in between your studies so take this into account when choosing your provider. What is the nightlife like? How far is it from home? What is the culture like? Where would you live in relation to the college? What are the pubs and restaurants like? Could you imagine yourself living there? If you are a self-funded LPC student, you might like to consider providers close to home so that you can save money. Also think about where you would like to practise. Providers generally have close links with the local legal profession, which provides a good opportunity to make contacts in the area in which you wish to practise.

9. **Additional qualifications**—some providers give non-law LPC graduates the opportunity to "top up" to an LLB award (law degree) if they have completed both the GDL and LPC with them. Some providers also offer the opportunity for LPC graduates to "top up" to an LLM (Masters in Law) by completing some additional units and writing a dissertation. Contact individual providers for more information if these options appeal to you.

As part of your research, you should visit providers' websites and make an effort to attend open days to get a feel for the culture of the institution and find out more about the surrounding area. Also speak to representatives from LPC providers at law fairs and students who have already completed, or are currently enrolled on, the course. If you manage to secure work experience or vacation schemes, take the opportunity to speak to current trainees about their experiences of the LPC and any advice they would give you when choosing a provider. You might also like to look at the profiles on *www.targetcourses.co.uk/home/*.

Think very carefully before embarking on the LPC. Getting a training contract is a very competitive process and there is no guarantee of getting one just because you complete the LPC.

A Trainee Solicitor

Some of the people on my course just didn't seem to realise that there is no guarantee of a training contract at the end of it.

A Trainee Solicitor

Applying for the LPC

Some universities have entered into agreements with particular LPC providers to give their students a guaranteed place on the LPC programme and some LPC providers offer discounted fees for students who complete both the GDL and LPC with them. It is worth checking with your university and LPC provider to find out about such schemes.

Regardless of where you intend to study, applications for the full time LPC must be made via the Central Applications Board. You can download a sample application form from the website (*www.lawcabs.ac.uk/*). You can apply to up to three providers and will be asked to list them in order of preference. You will also need to arrange for a tutor to provide an academic reference by email.

The application process opens on October 1 each year. If you wish to be considered in the initial selection stage (ending at the end of March in each year), your application form and academic reference must be received by the Central Application Board no later than December 1 in the year before you wish to begin the course. So, if you wish to start the course in September 2011, your application form must be received by December 1, 2010 to be considered in the first round. Applications received after December 1 (but before the end of the first round of applications) will be considered at the end of March. Check the website for further details of the application process and to ensure that the submission dates have not changed.

Applications for part time or distance learning courses should be made directly to the individual institution.

Important notes

1. The exemptions from the academic stage of training granted under the GDL or qualifying law degree remain valid for seven years from the date of graduation so you must complete the LPC within this period.

2. Before you begin the LPC, you must register as a student member of the Solicitors Regulation Authority (SRA) **and** obtain confirmation from them that you have completed the academic stage of training to become a solicitor. If you have not done this, you will not be able to commence the LPC or your training contract. The fee for registration is £110 for 2010 entry. Applications and registration fees must be submitted no later than August 1 in the year in which you wish to begin the LPC (subject to note 3 below).

   If you have applied through the Central Applications Board, you will automatically be sent an application form for student membership of the SRA. If you do not receive this form by mid-March in the year in which you wish to begin the LPC, you should contact the SRA directly:

   Information Services
   The Solicitors Regulation Authority
   Ipsley Court
   Berrington Close
   Redditch
   Worcestershire
   B98 0TD
   Telephone: 0870 606 2555
   Fax: 0207 320 5964
   email: *info.services@sra.org.uk*

3. For the purposes of applying for student membership of the SRA, your law degree or GDL will only remain valid for a period of

seven years from October 1 of the year in which the degree is awarded.

4. As part of your application for student membership of the SRA, you will be asked to declare any matters that may affect your suitability to become a solicitor. This includes matters such as criminal convictions, warnings, cautions and reprimands (even if they are spent), instances of plagiarism or cheating, declarations of bankruptcy, County Court judgments against you, evidence that you are unable to manage your financial affairs, and anything else that may call into question your character. If any character or suitability issues need to be considered as part of your application, you must ensure that your application and registration fee are submitted by April 1 in the year in which you wish to begin the LPC.

5. If you have failed units in the final year of your degree or the GDL course and need to re-sit the assessments, you may still apply for student membership of the SRA (before August 1) but you must notify them of your position and inform them of the results of your re-sit assessments by October 31. If you fail a re-sit and are required to leave the LPC course, you can apply for a refund of your student membership fee. Contact the SRA directly for more information on this process.

6. Law graduates and GDL graduates who have completed their course at a single institution and have passed all the foundation subjects will have their names passed to the SRA in a block certificate by their university or college in the summer before the LPC begins. This is known as the certificate of completion of the academic stage of training. However, if you completed your law degree at more than one institution, you will need to give the SRA a transcript giving complete details of the course of your studies. This means that you will need to get in touch with the relevant institutions to provide separate academic transcripts and ask them to certify that the relevant foundation subjects have been studied and passed. If your degree was awarded a year or more before you apply for the LPC, your name will not be included on the block certificate for that year so you should include a copy of your academic transcript with your application form.

For further information on any of the above guidance notes and to check that the key deadlines have not changed, you should refer to the relevant pages of the SRA website (*http://www.sra.org.uk/students/student-enrolment.page*).

Tips for success on the LPC

1. Keep on top of the work from the very beginning and do not be tempted to miss classes. While you may not find the work conceptually challenging, the volume is fairly high, particularly when coursework is due. Therefore, you must manage your time effectively and not allow work to mount up.

It's not difficult; it's the quantity of work and managing your time that can be challenging. The people on my LPC course who didn't attend all their classes were the ones who didn't pass.

A Trainee Solicitor

2. Do not ignore the preparation for workshops. This is a key part of the learning process and you will not be able to catch up by cramming at the end of the course.

In some respects, the LPC is quite good preparation for life as a trainee. It's not like university; you can't just turn up to a seminar and not say anything. You are expected to contribute and to have read the preparatory materials and thought about your answers, which is similar to what it is like when you are asked to present something to a partner or an associate during the training contract. It forces you to work on your organisational skills, be prepared, and think about what sort of issues are likely to come up.

Ben Wheeler, Trainee Solicitor, Berwin Leighton Paisner LLP

3. Many students find that the most effective way to manage the LPC workload is to adopt a practice of working between 9am and 5pm every day. This is good preparation for the world of work, which is now not too far away—although you can expect much longer hours in real life! Of course, you will have to be prepared to work extra hours during exam periods or in the run up to coursework

submission dates but, on the whole, it should be possible to balance a full working day with plenty of time for socialising.

A lot of people describe the LPC as more like a job and that can be a shock after university. You have to prepare the checklists and condense the manuals into something that is manageable. It's really all about a consistent level of working week after week.

Claire Walls, Trainee Solicitor, Berwin Leighton Paisner LLP

4. Do not ignore your future career. If you have not yet secured a training contract, use the year to make contacts and network. Attend all careers events and law fairs and take advantage of any application workshops or mock interview services offered by your provider.

5. Take advantage of any Pro Bono opportunities and/or other extra-curricular activities. It is important to continue to develop your CV and make contacts within the profession, particularly if you have not yet secured a training contract.

6. Do not be fooled by open book exams and multiple choice questions. As with all good multiple choice questions, you still need to know the topic in depth if you are to have any chance of success and each possible answer will be very similar to the next. You will not have time to search for an answer in the materials; they are there as a quick reference tool and you need to have sufficient knowledge to use them effectively.

7. This is the beginning of your future career so adopt a professional attitude at all times. You never know who might prove to be a useful contact in the future.

11 THE TRAINING CONTRACT

After you have completed the LPC, you will need to complete a training contract in order to qualify as a solicitor. The training contract lasts for two years and is generally divided into four "seats" of six months which are spent in different practice areas, although some firms offer a greater number of shorter seats. The training contract provides trainees with a broad training base and the opportunity to experience different practice areas before deciding where they would like to qualify.

The Solicitors Regulation Authority (SRA) states that you need to have good experience of at least three different practice areas during the course of your training contract. It does not specify how long you must spend in each department but suggests that the equivalent of three months would be necessary to gain appropriate experience. The training contract must also span both contentious and non-contentious work.

It is possible to complete the training contract on a part time basis provided that the contract is completed within a four year period and that the trainee works at least two and a half days each week. Look at the SRA guidelines on part time training contracts if this is something that is of interest to you (*www.sra.org.uk/students/training-contract.page*).

The training contract can be reduced on account of previous legal experience obtained in the three years immediately before the training contract begins. This is subject to the agreement of the training contract provider and the maximum reduction that can be secured is six months (based on 12 months of experience).

During your training contract you must complete the Professional Skills Course (PSC), with a provider who is accredited by the SRA. Your firm will fund this course for you and give you paid time off to attend the training sessions and assessments. The PSC consists of three core modules (Client Care and Professional Standards, Advocacy and Communication Skills, and Financial and Business Skills) and additional elective modules. Some firms choose to send their trainees on an intensive course, while others spread the modules over the course of the training contract.

Wherever you decide to train, your training will have to meet requirements set down by the SRA. For further details of these requirements, visit the student pages of the SRA website (*www.sra.org.uk/students/ students.page*).

Where Can I Train?

The most obvious place to train and work as a solicitor is within a law firm, but your options are certainly not limited solely to law firms. For example, you might decide to train as a solicitor with the Crown Prosecution Service, or a local authority, or with the in-house legal team of a large corporation. This is a serious decision, which will determine the direction of your future career so make sure you engage in serious research to find out what type of organisation would suit you best and expose you to the areas of practice that you are interested in.

Money was not a factor that I thought about when I chose law as a career. Obviously it's nice to have that security there and I'm probably earning more than my friends are but that's not why I do it. You have to enjoy the work first and foremost.

A Trainee Solicitor at a City Firm

Section 5 provides an overview of different types of law firm and explores various practice areas. It also discusses some alternative training contract providers to illustrate the breadth of opportunities that are available outside the traditional law firm environment.

How to Get the Most out of Your Training Contract

Putting academic credentials aside for a moment, what makes a good trainee and how can you get the most out of your training contract? No two trainees are the same, but there are certain attributes that some of the best trainees have in common.

1. Keep an open mind when starting each new seat. Commercial property might not be your ideal practice area, but the people in

your department have chosen to make a career there; do not insult them by moaning every time you are given work, or by making it clear that you are only there to "tick a box" before moving onto a more interesting area of practice. Equally, a training contract can be full of surprises: you might find that the land law you hated at university suddenly becomes fascinating in the context of commercial property deals. It has also been known for even the most narrow-minded of trainees to forget his prejudices towards a particular seat when he is desperately seeking a permanent position on qualification so do not burn your bridges.

As I approach qualification, my qualification choices have changed partly as a result of changes in the market and the availability of jobs, which meant that I have had to consider other options. My advice would be to try to keep an open mind and work hard in each seat. In today's market, you have to have four good appraisals otherwise even the department that you perform excellently in won't take you on because the competition is so strong.

A Trainee Solicitor at a City firm

2. Adopt a positive attitude. It is far nicer to work with positive people rather than those who do not integrate and make it clear that they would rather be somewhere else. Loyalty to the firm and to your department can go a long way and might be the key to successful retention if there is a choice between you and another candidate on qualification.

3. Respect and be courteous to everyone. You never know who you are going to need in the future. Even if you are certain that you will not want to qualify into a seat, you might well find yourself working in larger, cross departmental teams with many of those solicitors in the future and, therefore, forming good relationships during your training contract will pay dividends in the end. Also, never underestimate the support staff who will often know far more about a particular practice area than you can possibly imagine. They will also be able to help you with practical issues such as ordering stationery, finding templates on the computer system, and showing you how to record and bill time to particular

clients. Life will be far more difficult for you if you do not make an effort to form a good relationship with them from the outset.

4. Support your fellow trainees. You will find that they provide a source of much needed encouragement and guidance during your training contract. They know just how frightening that partner in commercial litigation can be, and they probably have a template disclosure letter that you might need when your supervisor asks you to prepare one at short notice on your first day in a new seat, they can probably also give you some tips on how to sweet talk the difficult secretary in the family law team, and will bring you a coffee and sandwich when you have been asked to check a stack of verification notes and will not make it home before midnight. However, remember that it is a two-way process and you need to invest in them too.

5. Work hard in every seat. The hard work does not end once you have secured the training contract. From then on, you have to prove that you can survive in the real world and persuade senior colleagues that you are worthy of a permanent position on qualification. Quite often firms will judge you on your performance in your least favourite seat as an indicator of your strength of character and professionalism. We all have to do jobs we do not like from time to time, but firms want people who are happy to roll up their sleeves and get on with the task in hand.

We often judge people on how they cope in the seat that we know is not one they particularly want to do because that is a good indicator of how they will cope in difficult times.
                                        Malcolm Padgett, Training Partner, Coffin Mew LLP

6. Be enthusiastic and maintain a sense of humour. You will be given some difficult tasks to complete during your training contract ranging from the excruciatingly boring (e.g. proof reading 100 leases or scheduling bundles of completion documents) to the downright frightening (e.g. your first solo completion meeting or client interview). A sense of humour and thick skin will help see you through, and remember every job has its drawbacks and one day you will be able to delegate these tasks to another unsuspecting trainee!

7. Know when to ask for help and when to use your initiative. Your supervisor will not mind you asking questions (that is the whole point of having a supervisor), but you must learn quickly how to get the right balance between using your initiative and seeking advice from others. There will be times when your supervisor is not available to answer your question. In that case you will need to do your own research, look back over the correspondence to see if you can find the answer to your question, or perhaps ask another colleague.

It can be difficult to know where the boundaries lie when dealing with clients because different supervisors have very different expectations. You can spend several months with someone who prefers to limit your exposure to clients and then move to sit with someone who wants you to do everything. It can make you question yourself.

A Trainee Solicitor

If in doubt, ask someone. I felt a very strong pressure to show that I could do everything already. Although people do respect your ability to take the initiative, you don't always have to do that and there are some things where you should check whether it's OK to send something out. You don't have to go straight in and say 'I don't know what to do', but you could offer some solutions or options and ask how they would like you to proceed.

A Trainee Solicitor

It's far better to get told off because you happen to be knocking on someone's door at the wrong time, rather than make a huge mistake that could result in a law suit. I've had a couple of experiences where partners have been a bit short with me but they usually come back later and apologise for it. You can't take things too personally.

A Trainee Solicitor

8. Do not be too sensitive. Lawyers are often forced to work very long hours under extremely pressurised conditions and this can make people short tempered and intolerant. Do not take this personally, just get on with the job and know when to keep quiet.

Equally, learn how to take criticism constructively and to reflect on the strengths and weaknesses of your performance at work. If you make a mistake or are given advice on how to improve your performance in a particular area, take it in and learn from it. If you were expected to be the perfect solicitor from day one, there would be no need for the training contract.

One day you can have a great day and everything goes well and the next day you can feel completely useless.

A Trainee Solicitor

On my first day in a new seat, I sent out an invoice that had been prepared by the previous trainee relating to a file I had inherited from him. The client was furious and made things very difficult for me. It was difficult to learn how to deal with that even though I knew I had done nothing wrong. You just have to learn to rise above it.

A Trainee Solicitor

9. Try to think commercially. This is a difficult one for trainees, many of whom will arrive fresh from university and law school, but it is one of the keys to a successful career. Make an effort to think about the commercial context of a particular transaction or instruction and discuss it with your supervisor. Also, make an effort to keep up to date with current and financial affairs and think about how they impact on clients' businesses and/or the projects you are working on. Even if you are not going to specialise in commercial law, you will need to keep in mind that solicitors are there to make money for their firms and to learn the importance of effective time recording and timely billing—this is as much about commercial awareness as anything else.

10. Manage your time and remain organised. As a trainee you might find yourself working for several different people in the same department and this can sometimes lead to problems with balancing conflicting interests. Although you must show that you can cope with competing demands on your time and are able to manage your workload effectively, this is a skill to be developed over time and you should always feel that you can ask for support

from your supervisor. At the very least you should keep people informed of progress on a particular file and do not wait until the last minute before asking for help or telling them that you are not going to be able to complete the work within the timeframe. If you really cannot get something completed by a deadline, consider asking another trainee to help you (if your supervisor is happy with that).

Make a note of key dates and deadlines on files and do not be afraid to remind your supervisor of them if you think he has forgotten. They are only human too and can sometimes forget things and, even if they have remembered, they will probably be very impressed to see that you have used your initiative.

Keep an up-to-date record of all the files you are working on, including the particular tasks you have been allocated for each one and the relevant deadlines. This will help you prioritise matters and manage your time and it will be useful when other fee earners ask about your capacity to help with a new matter, or if your supervisor asks for an update on your workload. It will also act as a useful record of the work you have been involved in during your training contract.

11. Always carry a pen and notebook to meetings. This might sound obvious but it is such an important part of being a good trainee and it is amazing how many people forget to do this.

Never go into someone's room without taking a pen and paper. Even if you are just popping in for a chat, you can come out with a load of new instructions!

A Trainee Solicitor

12. Accept that it will take time to settle into each new seat. Many trainees find it rather unsettling to move between seats but this is an inevitable part of the training process so you need to learn to deal with it.

One of the biggest challenges of the training contract is moving seats because you've just got comfortable, everyone knows you and what you are capable of, they know they can trust you and then you have to go somewhere else in the firm and start again. You also have to get to know the culture and working practices of the new department and how they like things done.

Rebecca Brown, Trainee Solicitor, Coffin Mew LLP

I was in corporate for my first seat and it was such a sea change moving to my real estate seat where you are really thrown in at the deep end. In real estate you're running files from day one and suddenly you've got all these calls and emails coming in from clients whereas in corporate you stand behind maybe two or three people up the food chain from you.

Jonathan Pugh-Smith, Trainee Solicitor, Berwin Leighton Paisner LLP

The biggest challenge of my training contract so far has been accepting that, just as I am settling into my first seat, I have to move to another department and start again. Rotating seats keeps you on your toes and prevents you from getting too settled.

Moira Campbell, Trainee Solicitor, Kingsley Napley

13. Learn to deal with sleepless nights. If you are thinking of specialising in corporate or banking work, you need to learn how to operate effectively on very little sleep.

Unless you are really lucky, there are going to be points where you will go home at 2 o'clock in the morning and come back in at 9 o'clock for about a week.

Philippa Chatterton, Solicitor, Freshfields

14. Get used to being out of your comfort zone for much of the time. The training contract provides a steep learning curve and you will often be asked to carry out tasks at short notice with very little background knowledge.

One of my most challenging experiences as a trainee was when I said I would cover for a trainee who was going on holiday and help with a completion meeting. I was responsible for all the document management on a huge multi-jurisdictional deal. It started on Friday and we completed the following Thursday at 3am.

A Trainee Solicitor at a City Firm

Qualification

Upon qualification, many trainees will be offered posts by their firm, although this is dependent on market conditions at the time and should not be assumed to be a guaranteed outcome. When deciding which area to qualify into, you need to reflect honestly on your performance in each of your seats and what you want to achieve from your career in the long term. Think about your wider career aspirations; where you would like to be in ten years time; the type of clients you want to work for; the culture of particular departments; the type of work you enjoyed most during your training; how much money you want to earn; and perhaps also how important family and leisure time is to you.

For some trainees, the last few months of the training contract can be a very stressful time indeed. While for many the transition from trainee to newly qualified solicitor seems to work out seamlessly, others will face an uncertain future as they find that they are not being retained by their firm or that there are no positions available in the department of their choice. If you find yourself in this position, you need to keep an open mind, remain positive, have faith in your ability and, above all, keep going. Hopefully, you will have taken the advice given above and approached all your seats with a positive attitude and an open mind. This will at least put you in the best possible position when it comes to selection.

12 BEYOND QUALIFICATION

Time for Celebrations

At the end of the long and, for many, very expensive road of studying and training is the prize of being admitted to the roll of solicitors. Once you have completed your training contract, as long as you have passed the Professional Skills Course and have obtained a satisfactory standard disclosure from the Criminal Records Bureau, you will be admitted to the roll and issued with your first practising certificate.

It can seem rather surreal to arrive in the office on your first day as a qualified solicitor and wonder what really is so different to yesterday! The first few months as a newly qualified solicitor can be daunting and rather stressful as you adjust to life as a professional and start taking responsibility for your own workload and clients. Take things slowly and remember that you are not expected to be running your own practice immediately. You can, and should, still ask senior colleagues for guidance. One of the most rewarding aspects of this career is the continual learning curve so you are not expected to know it all on day one!

Try to build up a broad range of work experience during your first few years as a qualified solicitor and, if possible, work with several different solicitors or partners. This will ensure that you have plenty of inspiration when developing your own approach to practice and client management and the more varied your workload, the more confident you will be when dealing with new matters in the future.

You will be invited to attend an admissions ceremony (normally some months after actually qualifying) to celebrate your achievement with family and friends. Do make every effort to attend this ceremony. It is a wonderful achievement to have qualified as a solicitor so enjoy the limelight for a couple of hours at least before the hard work begins again!

Continuing Professional Development

One of the most challenging and stimulating aspects of a career as a solicitor is the fact that you never seem to stop learning. There will be legal reforms to keep on top of and political and regulatory developments to take into account. This is reflected in the requirement for full time practising solicitors to complete a minimum of 16 hours continuing professional development each year (there are reduced requirements for those working fewer than 32 hours per week). These hours can be satisfied by a combination of internal and external training sessions and courses and it is not difficult to satisfy this requirement. Make sure you keep an up to date record of the courses that you attend each year.

SECTION 4: GAINING EXPERIENCE AND ENHANCING YOUR CV

13 THE IMPORTANCE OF "NETWORKING"

What is Networking?

Networking is establishing a network or circle of professional relationships—people you would be able to email and ask questions of. The way that you make first contact with these people can be incredibly varied but students need to be ready to take down names and email addresses and to think about how the contact could develop. It won't always work, but the worst that can happen is someone will say that they can't help because they are too busy.

Veronica Oldfield, Careers Consultant and Tutor, College of Law

There is no place for modesty or shyness when it comes to applying for training contracts. The marketplace is incredibly competitive and effective networking is essential to a successful outcome. This is your chance to showcase your skills and demonstrate your motivation to become a solicitor. Never miss an opportunity to ask for work experience or to speak to someone about their career path and any advice they could offer you. As long as you are courteous and professional, the worst that can happen is that they will say that they cannot help you. However, you will often find that people are only too happy to talk to you because they remember how difficult it was when they were trying to secure a training contract.

One of my students had a weekend job at a hair salon and managed to secure work experience by approaching one of the clients. He was a solicitor and took an interest in her because he was impressed by her perseverance and powers of persuasion. It's essential to make the most of every single contact because you never know where they might lead you.

Cheryl Keal, Careers Advisor, University of Portsmouth

Networking does not end once you have secured a training contract; it is an increasingly important aspect of legal practice in its own right. Therefore, recruiters want to know that you will be a good ambassador for their firm and that you will have the confidence and skills to attend business development events to win new work and clients, and raise your firm's profile. They will have this in mind when they meet you at interviews, assessment days, or other careers events.

Networking Events

Your university or GDL/LPC provider might arrange networking events for you. These could consist of guest lectures, careers workshops, law fairs, drinks receptions, or mentoring schemes. You should make every effort to attend these events. The guests will be volunteers who have given up their time to help students with career planning and this will make the networking process even easier—they are there to help you so it will not be as difficult as trying to warm up cold contacts.

The application process starts before you even pick up an application form: go to the careers fairs; do your research beforehand and target firms carefully; introduce yourself to representatives from your chosen firms and tell them that you want to work for their firm and why. Create a positive impression there. In short, you must take every opportunity to meet the recruitment people so that when your application arrives, those firms will recognise who you are. It's this level of pro-activity that convinces me that you have a genuine interest in working for my firm. Also, make sure you actually make reference to these meetings in your application and follow up on any offers of help—if there is a half open door, push it open (it's amazing how many students fail to follow up on these meetings or make use of my contact details if I give them a business card).

Kevin Chard, Training Manager, Blake Lapthorn

It is fair to say that effective networking comes more naturally to some people than others. Nonetheless, it is a skill that can be developed if you persevere. It really is worth the effort to develop this invaluable business tool and it does get easier the more you do it.

Tips for effective networking

1. Before you attend an event, take some time to think about why you are going, who you would like to speak to, and why you wish to speak with them.

2. First impressions count so pay attention to your appearance. If possible, check the dress code beforehand but, if you are in any doubt about what to wear, it is usually safest to dress up rather than down. Recruiters will be looking for people who know how to dress appropriately in a business environment and who will give a polished and professional appearance when introduced to clients or prospective clients. Seemingly small details can make all the difference so make sure that your shoes are polished, your nails and hair are neat, your clothes are pressed, and any jewellery is kept to a minimum.

3. Consider eating before an event so that you do not have to worry about holding a conversation while balancing a plate of food and a drink.

4. Arrive early to avoid the fear of entering a large crowd of people. If you do arrive to a packed room, take a deep breath and look out for someone who is on their own. They will probably be just as relieved to speak to someone as you are. If everyone seems to be in groups already, make your way to a busy area such as the drinks table or registration area and try to break into a group of people who have also just arrived. This should make it easier to start a conversation, rather than trying to break into a group where conversation is already well established. Remember that everyone else is in the same boat and you will be surprised at how easy it is to make conversation once you have attended a couple of these events.

5. Never underestimate the impact of a firm handshake and a warm smile. When you meet or are introduced to someone, always shake his hand and maintain eye contact.

6. Prepare a short introduction to use when you meet someone new. This will give you confidence and ensure that you make a positive first impression. Do not waste the opportunity by simply giving your name; tell the other person something about yourself and perhaps why you are attending this particular event.

7. Although it can be tempting to attend an event with a friend, this can sometimes be counter-productive if you cling to each other

nervously and fail to embrace the opportunity to make new contacts.

8. Make people feel valued when they are speaking to you. Do not cast your eyes around the room to see if there is anyone else worth speaking to. Make an effort to be attentive and ask questions to show that you are interested in what they are telling you. If you really do not feel that the conversation is going anywhere, you can excuse yourself politely after a reasonable time.

9. Always follow up any contacts as soon as possible after the event.

10. If you find it difficult to start conversations with people and to engage in "small talk", it can help to practise speaking to strangers, for example, when you are shopping or waiting for the bus. Try to speak to one new person each day; you will be amazed at how much easier and more natural the process becomes with a little practice. Also make an effort to keep up to date with the latest news stories and read a quality newspaper regularly to avoid being caught out if the conversation turns to current affairs. This will also help if you run out of things to talk about as you can think about a few topics in advance to fall back on if the conversation dries up at any point.

You have to make the most of every contact. If you meet trainees at networking events or other careers events and they give you their card, make sure you follow it up and don't be afraid to ask for some help or guidance when it comes to preparing your application forms. As long as you don't overstep the mark, they are likely to be the kind of people who are happy to help applicants because they've volunteered for these careers events.

A Law Undergraduate

14 WORK EXPERIENCE

Why is Work Experience so Important?

Although the prospect of applying for work experience might seem daunting and time consuming, the rewards are more than worth the effort. For students, even a short period of work experience provides an insight into the day-to-day working life of individuals within the profession. It will also help you determine whether or not you have the skills and motivation to get through the training and survive as a qualified solicitor. Finally, it will ensure that you are not an anonymous application when you apply; the recruitment partners or managers will have had first-hand experience of your abilities. They will have seen how you perform in a work environment and therefore will be able to make an informed decision about whether or not to employ you. Many firms ultimately offer training contracts to students who attended vacation schemes with them.

> I think the most important piece of advice for aspiring solicitors is to get some work experience. First of all, it helps you get a better idea of the type of firm you want to work for and, secondly, it can be a real foot in the door to get a training contract with that firm. In such a competitive environment, if you've visited a firm and they know who you are then they are more likely (if they like you) to invite you back because it's easier for them. They can put a face to the application, and they've seen how you perform in the workplace.
>
> *Rebecca Brown, Trainee Solicitor, Coffin Mew LLP*

Employers expect to see evidence of work experience on your CV. It reassures them of your commitment, demonstrates an appreciation of the realities of a career in law, and shows that you have made an informed decision to pursue this career path. When you apply for training contracts, you will be asked "Why do you want to be a solicitor?" and "Why do you want to work for a firm like this one?". Work experience will help you formulate answers to those questions and will demonstrate that you are a motivated individual who has been willing to invest time and effort to further your career.

We are looking for people who have considered the full range of training contract opportunities from Magic Circle firms all the way through to spending a couple of days with their local council's legal team. Perhaps they have also shadowed a judge or spent a day in chambers. In any event, they have explored all avenues available to them and then re-focused on a firm like ours.

Malcolm Padgett, Training Partner, Coffin Mew LLP

You need to be able to demonstrate that you understand the workings of a law firm and have made an informed decision to follow this career path . . . legal work experience is invaluable in that regard.

Amanda Danvers, Solicitor, Shoosmiths

Legal work experience is not the only way to make yourself attractive to employers; there are many other forms of valuable work experience and other ways of enhancing your CV. These are discussed in more detail in Chs 17 and 18. Nonetheless, firms will expect to see *some* evidence of legal work placements and it is in your interest to secure the broadest possible range of experiences to show that you have considered all avenues and made an informed decision about the type of firm or organisation you would like to train with.

You might find that you do not actually enjoy your work experience and realise that you do not want to be a solicitor after all. This is an equally valuable outcome: it is much better to make this decision before you invest considerable time and money in the GDL or LPC. You will also have a good idea of what you want to avoid in other career options, which should make your research easier.

Work experience is the only way you can find out what will suit you. If you can get work experience before your vacation schemes then that will help but, if not, try to use your vacation schemes to work out whether that type of career or firm will suit you because studying the law is so different to actually working in it. Even if you love the law degree, you might hate legal practice and vice versa. Also don't forget that it's a really broad profession and there will be areas of law and legal practice that you haven't even studied at university.

Jo Pennick, Third Year Law Undergraduate, King's College London

Legal work experience can be divided into a number of different categories:

1. Informal unpaid work experience.

2. Formal vacation schemes (see Ch.15).

3. Open days.

4. Paralegal experience.

5. Pro bono activities (see Ch.16).

Informal Work Experience

Students used to be able to write directly to firms and arrange ad hoc periods of work experience during the holidays. While this is still the case with some of the smaller high street firms and public sector employers, larger firms have formalised their work experience programmes so that they have become almost as difficult to secure as vacation schemes and training contracts. So, how can you maximise your chances of securing work experience?

Sometimes universities and LPC providers run internal competitions where the first prize is a period of work experience with a local firm of solicitors. You should seriously consider entering such competitions: you will have a new skill to add to your CV and there is the prospect of work experience if you win.

If you decide to write to firms to arrange work experience, you should be flexible in terms of the length of the placement and who you will be working with. Your letter should be no more than one side of A4 and will need to be targeted towards each individual firm. You should explain what you hope to gain from the experience, your background and future career plans, and why you are particularly interested in working for that firm. The letter should enclose a copy of your CV which, ideally, should not span more than two sides of A4. It is a good idea to call the firm beforehand and find out who your letter should be addressed to (it will usually either be the partner in charge of training or a human resources advisor). Ch.24 provides more detailed guidance on how to write an effective CV and covering letter.

Do not be too fussy about the level of contact that is offered to you. If someone offers to meet with you for an informal chat about your career, accept their offer and see where it leads. A short meeting after work or a series of email exchanges might eventually lead to a work experience opportunity or an introduction to another useful contact.

In the early stages, try asking to shadow someone, rather than suggesting work experience. That's a lot less to ask for and is often more acceptable in the eyes of a busy solicitor. You will need to be brave and have a go at 'networking'—speak to friends of friends, neighbours, law tutors, etc. Another option is to write a speculative letter asking for work experience, although this must be a well written, targeted letter explaining why you would like to spend time getting experience in that particular firm or legal department and in that particular type of work.

Veronica Oldfield, Careers Consultant and Tutor, College of Law

I know a couple of people who rang up the graduate recruitment people at a particular firm and asked if they could go in and speak to them. I'm sure not every firm will do that but it might be worth picking up the phone to see if you can get in and speak to somebody.

A Trainee Solicitor

Make the most of any contacts and do not make the mistake of thinking that this only means senior partners or graduate recruitment managers at law firms. Quite often junior members of staff will be just as helpful and they are likely to have more time available to spend with you. Also, do not be too fussy about the content of the work experience. The most important factor is often not what you did, but how effectively you "sell" the experience to prospective employers.

Don't underestimate any contact or period of work experience, however insignificant it might seem. I didn't have any contacts in the profession but my friend's Mum was a personal injury lawyer so I did some work experience with her and put together a database of recent claims and percentage success rates. Even that gave me something to talk about at interviews although the work wasn't actually relevant to a City firm.

A Trainee Solicitor at a City Firm

Try to be creative in your quest to secure work experience and think beyond applications to law firms. For example, if you are interested in property law, consider writing to the planning department of your local council to see if you could spend a few days or weeks shadowing someone in their team. You might be able to carry out research, accompany officers on inspections or attend planning meetings, which will give you exposure to the wider context within which property transactions are completed. Public sector organisations are very often under resourced so they might be grateful for longer term support if you express an interest in their work.

If you are interested in family law, you could consider becoming a student member of Resolution (*www.resolution.org.uk*). This is a voluntary organisation which campaigns for improvements in family law and the family justice system. Its focus is on a constructive, non-confrontational approach to the resolution of family problems. It also supports students who are interested in qualifying as family lawyers. LPC students who are taking the family law elective are eligible for one year's free membership. This means that you will be entitled to discounts on training courses, a regular family law newsletter, and access to the members' website.

If you are interested in intellectual property law, you could consider spending time working for a trade mark or patent attorney. Alternatively, you might be able to secure work experience with the brand protection or marketing team of a company to learn about key intellectual property concerns from a commercial client's perspective.

If you are interested in a career in public service, you could consider volunteering at your local Trading Standards office or Citizens Advice Bureaux. You could also consider working for a Law Centre or mediation service in your local area. Opportunities for work experience in the not-for-profit sector are considered in more detail in Ch.16.

Open Days

Some firms run Open Days as a way of getting a large number of prospective trainees to visit the firm on one day, rather than running weeks of work experience programmes. The Open Days are usually offered in addition to formal vacation schemes, although sometimes they are part of the application process leading to a place on such schemes.

Open Days provide an opportunity to visit a firm and speak to members of its staff (generally trainee solicitors, the graduate recruitment manager and perhaps also one or two of the recruitment partners). An Open Day provides an excellent opportunity to get a feel for the culture of a firm, to find out more about the structure and quality of its training contract, and to make a positive impression on the key decision makers.

Generally speaking, Open Days involve a tour of the offices, a talk by the recruitment partner or graduate recruitment manager, an opportunity to meet and ask questions of members of staff (often over lunch or coffee), and perhaps also a group exercise which will be good practice for assessment centres and vacation schemes. You will need to look at firms' websites to find exact details of what to expect from their Open Days and how to apply. You should also find out whether they will reimburse your travel expenses.

Why should you attend an Open Day?

1. You can mention attendance at Open Days in the work experience section of your CV. It shows that you have used your initiative and are motivated to find out more about the legal recruitment process and career opportunities.

2. Attending Open Days is a very effective and efficient way of gathering information about the culture and working environment of individual firms. You are able to spend time in their offices and meet key members of staff but the whole visit is over in one day.

3. Open Days are a great way to make contacts and they provide an opportunity to create a positive impression on those involved in the recruitment process.

When filling out applications, it is difficult to answer the question "Why do you want to work for our firm in particular?". An open day can be very useful for this because you will actually have something to say. You will know a little about the firm and you can mention the open day on your application form.

Elena Gubay, Law Undergraduate,
King's College London

Tips for Open Days

1. Make sure that you arrive on time (if not a bit early).

2. Think carefully about your appearance. You should wear a suit and make sure that your shoes are polished and your hair, nails, and any accessories are neat and appropriate for a business environment.

3. First impressions are crucial. Never underestimate the power of a firm handshake, a warm smile, and a confident (but not arrogant) demeanour.

4. Take Open Days seriously and treat them as part of the recruitment process. Maintain a professional attitude throughout the day and be polite to everyone you meet, regardless of their status within the firm. Feedback will be given at the end of each event and you do not want to be remembered as the one who over indulged in the wine or was rude to the receptionist on arrival.

5. Mix with the other candidates as well as the firm's employees. Recruiters will be interested to see how you respond to your peers and how confidently you can navigate a networking event.

6. Research the firm before the event and, if possible, find out about the background of any important individuals who will be attending, e.g. the graduate recruitment manager and any partners.

7. Read a quality newspaper regularly and make sure that you are well informed about current affairs to avoid being caught out. For Open Days at City firms and other commercial firms, make sure that you read the financial pages regularly and are well informed about economic issues, recent deals, and financial news stories.

8. Think of questions to ask but remember that your question will reveal a lot about you. Do not ask something that you could find out easily by reviewing the firm's website or that shows you to be poorly informed about the legal recruitment process.

9. Read the guidance in Chs 13 and 27 on networking skills and assessment centre activities.

10. Send a thank you email after the event to acknowledge the effort
    that was invested in the day, and to remind the graduate recruit-
    ment manager of your name.

> Spend more time talking to the trainees than the partners. You won't be
> a partner for at least 10 years from where you are now. In fact, you may
> never become one. But you'll always have to start as a trainee so that's
> the perspective you should be interested in. Trainees also tend to be more
> open about the work environment of the firm.
>
>   *Simon Camilleri, LLB Law graduate, King's College London*

Paralegal Experience

> Paralegals provide legal support to solicitors. It is usually administrative
> work that can be distinguished from secretarial work. Paralegals are
> involved in a diverse range of tasks. In litigation departments, you can
> expect to prepare bundles, summarise disclosure, interview witnesses and
> carry out research.
>
>   *Moira Campbell, Trainee Solicitor, Kingsley Napley*

A paralegal is a non-lawyer who carries out legal work. They can work
in a variety of organisations, including law firms, local authorities,
in-house legal teams within large corporations, HM Court Service, and
the voluntary sector. The work of paralegals varies according to the type
of organisation they are working for. Duties could include carrying out
legal research, preparing legal documents and correspondence, instructing barristers, preparing court documents, interviewing clients or witnesses, taking notes of meetings or court hearings, and assisting with
general administrative duties.

You do not need any formal qualifications to become a paralegal,
although the Institute of Paralegals offers a qualification called the TPA
Certified Paralegal qualification. For more information on this qualification, you should visit the Institute of Paralegals website at *www
.instituteofparalegals.org*. As a general rule, employers will look for a
law graduate or someone who has completed the GDL. However, bear in
mind that many students apply for paralegal positions after the LPC if
they have not managed to secure a training contract so those who have
only completed the academic stage of training will be competing with

candidates who have a greater understanding of the practical application of law and legal transactions.

Many legal recruitment agencies find work for paralegals and most law schools keep a list of agencies and specialist recruiters in their career department. Some firms advertise vacancies on their website but some place adverts on legal careers websites or in the career departments of law schools. Sometimes it is also worth making speculative enquiries to firms that employ a large number of paralegals. If you have a very specific interest, but no relevant experience, it might be a good idea to offer to do work experience to begin with and see where it leads.

Moira Campbell, Trainee Solicitor, Kingsley Napley

Having finished the LPC without a training contract, I worked as a paralegal for 6 months at a firm of patent attorneys and then as a licensing assistant in a law firm for 6 months. Once I had some more experience, I found that I got quite a few interviews. The paralegal experience also gave me confidence at the beginning of the training contract and helped in terms of managing files, clients, workloads and professional relationships.

Rachael Williams, Solicitor, Coffin Mew LLP

Some people work as paralegals for many years, while for others it is a short term gap on the road to securing a training contract. Although paralegal experience is valued by firms, if your ultimate goal is to secure a training contract you should bear in mind that you do not want to be labelled as a career paralegal or as someone who, for whatever reason, cannot secure a training contract.

Paralegal experience can be good preparation for a training contract, but treat it as a short term post, rather than a long term solution, and be prepared for the fact that the pay can be extremely poor.

A Solicitor

15 VACATION SCHEMES: A FOOT IN THE DOOR

What are Vacation Schemes?

Vacation schemes are very good for gaining an insight into how different firms work and their individual cultures. They also give you a sense of what life as a trainee solicitor is actually like. You might find some aspects of the work surprisingly mundane; equally, you might find some things more interesting than you had expected. Once you know what lawyers do on a day-to-day basis, you have more of an idea of what firms are looking for and why. Most importantly, vacation schemes enable you to decide whether law is for you and which type of firm is likely to suit you before you sign up to your training contract. Given that the training contract plus LPC will take three years to complete, it's worth knowing what you actually want before you invest all this time in qualifying as a solicitor.

Elena Gubay, Law Undergraduate,
King's College London

Formal vacation schemes have replaced ad hoc work experience opportunities within most City, national and regional law firms. These firms run a series of work placements during the summer vacation (and sometimes also during the Christmas and Easter breaks) to give students the opportunity to find out more about their firms and what it is like to train and work there.

Many firms recruit heavily from students who have participated in their vacation schemes. Even if the schemes are not treated as a formal part of the recruitment process, they are an excellent way to find out more about a firm's culture, and to establish a relationship with the key decision makers. They provide an invaluable opportunity to see inside individual firms so you can get a good idea of what it would really be like to train and work there. By applying for, and participating in, vacation schemes you also demonstrate a genuine motivation to become a solicitor and show that you have made a concerted effort to find out more about the profession.

Vacation schemes are so important in terms of finding out about firms and whether you would actually want to work there. Don't lose sight of the fact that although they are working out whether they want to recruit you, it's also important to think about whether the firm is actually right for you.

Ben Wheeler, Trainee Solicitor, Berwin Leighton Paisner LLP

The Application Process

When selecting which firms to apply to, think about the type and size of the firm, the areas of law in which they specialise, and practical issues such as location. It is helpful to gain experience of as many different types of law firm as possible. As well as helping you to find out what type of firm you are best suited to, this is also useful when it comes to interviews and you are asked why you would like to train with that particular firm. You can show that you have made an informed decision having explored other types of firms and practice areas.

Competition for places on vacation schemes is fierce, especially amongst the larger law firms. Therefore, be prepared to apply for placements during the Christmas and Easter vacations, as well as the more popular summer schemes.

Since City firms and most national and regional firms recruit two years in advance, if you want to start your training contract straight after the LPC, you should apply for vacation schemes during your second year at university if you are a law undergraduate and during your third year for all other undergraduates. The deadlines for submitting applications for summer placements usually fall in January or February each year (although some remain open until April) and the deadlines for Christmas and Easter schemes are even earlier. Some firms use a single application form for vacation schemes and training contracts, while others run two separate application processes. You will need to research individual firms for exact details of their application processes and submission deadlines. The Chambers & Partners Student Guide to Becoming a Lawyer (*www.chambersstudent.co.uk*) has some useful information on applying for vacation schemes, including a timetable setting out the key deadlines.

What to Expect From Vacation Schemes

Even if you don't get a training contract as a result of the vacation scheme, you will learn a lot about working as a solicitor and whether that's the life for you.

A Vacation Scheme Student

Schemes usually last for between one and three weeks but the content of the placement varies from firm to firm. They generally involve a selection of the activities listed below.

1. Talks from partners or members of the graduate recruitment team.

2. Shadowing a trainee or junior solicitor and getting involved in fee earning work.

3. Research tasks.

4. Court visits.

5. Assessment centre activities.

6. Social events.

Remuneration varies: some firms pay their vacation scheme students (up to £400 per week at some US firms); others will reimburse reasonable travel expenses; and some do not offer any financial support.

Tips for Vacation Schemes

You've only got a week or so to make a good impression on a firm during your vacation scheme. Candidates stand out when they are genuinely engaged in the whole process and when they make a real effort to get on with everyone, from support staff to lawyers, and become part of the team. Try to be as natural and genuine as you possibly can. Roll your sleeves up and get involved in everything, including the social events.

Sam Lee, Graduate Recruitment Manager, Bond Pearce

Do not be distracted by the social events

You are there to make a positive impression on the recruiters, and to decide whether or not you could see yourself working for that firm. The firms are trying to impress you just as much as you are trying to impress them but it is possible to look passed the gloss and make a reasonable assessment of the culture, working practices and quality of training that the firm offers. Think about the rapport between the trainees and also between the trainees and senior members of staff. What is the working culture like? How supportive does the training environment seem to be? What hours do people work? What sort of work are trainees involved in? Do they cover the practice areas that you are interested in?

Personal qualities

Enthusiasm, confidence, the ability to build relationships and work as part of a team, and a proactive attitude are the qualities that are used most often to describe successful vacation scheme students.

Enthusiasm is a big factor to success on a vacation scheme. We take academic ability for granted but we're also looking for people with commercial awareness and an understanding of current affairs.
Ben Wheeler, Trainee Solicitor, Berwin Leighton Paisner LLP

Many applicants (particularly those applying to City firms) think that firms are looking for dominant, aggressive individuals. This is not the case. Do not feel that you have to adopt an aggressive personality or that you have to be incredibly domineering or always speak during negotiations or team building exercises. That is not what firms or clients want from their lawyers. Instead show that you are able to listen effectively as well as being able to drive things forward.

Although you are really focused and driven by what you are doing, you also need to be polite to others and supportive of their endeavours during the vacation scheme. Even though you want to succeed over others, you also need to show that you can build relationships and work as part of a team. If you are kind and generous towards others on the vacation scheme, it will reflect positively on you.
A Trainee Solicitor at a City Firm

Treat the scheme as an extended interview

Treat the scheme as if it were one long extended interview and remember that your performance is being assessed by those around you, even when you least expect it. With that point in mind, never underestimate the influence of current trainees.

Vacation scheme students shoot themselves in the foot when they are least expecting it to happen. In particular, they often under-estimate the role of the trainee in the recruitment process and the fact that we are asked to provide feedback on their performance in the workplace and socially. As much as you want them to be relaxed and confident, they have to remember that they are there to be assessed and that people are judging whether they are likely to fit into the culture of that particular firm.

A Trainee Solicitor at a City Firm

Show that you are a team player

You must maintain a professional attitude at all times: be courteous and respectful to everyone you meet, and take all tasks seriously. Those around you will be making an assessment about whether you have the potential to be a good trainee, whether you are likely to fit into the firm's culture, and whether you will be able to develop effective working relationships with colleagues and clients.

You need to show that you can work in a team with other people. Sometimes vacation scheme students can take over tasks and try to do everything themselves. You need to be proactive, but there is a balance to be struck.

Rachael Williams, Solicitor, Coffin Mew LLP

Concentrate on all tasks

It is not just the formal assessment centre tasks that are being assessed. Firms will be interested in how you perform in the workplace and how you approach the tasks that are allocated to you. Take every piece of work seriously and make sure you complete them within the agreed deadline.

Pay attention to presentation and do not be afraid to use your initiative if supplementary questions or issues arise out of the initial task.

Most firms will ask the supervisors to keep a record of the student's performance. In other words, don't mess around on the vacation scheme because it can be a two week interview.

A Law Undergraduate

A good candidate is someone who can be proactive when they get work to do and are able to "think on their feet". For example, if another task arises out of the initial instructions, be proactive and have a go at it.

Rebecca Brown, Trainee Solicitor, Coffin Mew LLP

The students who really distinguish themselves are those who take a pro-active approach to research tasks and are able to think laterally. They tend to go the extra mile to ask the natural supplementary question arising out of that research without actually being asked to consider it.

Jonathan Pugh-Smith, Trainee Solicitor, Berwin Leighton Paisner

You could have an individual who is really academic and able to carry out a piece of research competently, but if this isn't supplemented by soft skills and common sense (i.e. knowing when to ask questions, when to keep quiet or when to interrupt and suggest something), that individual is probably not going to stand out as much as someone who might have taken a bit longer to complete the research but always kept the fee earner informed and is personable, confident and able to use their initiative. In my opinion, that's often what makes people stand out.

Clare Reeve, Trainee Solicitor, Berwin Leighton Paisner LLP

Make sure that you attend all the social events, do not say that you have already made plans. People want to know that you are the kind of person who will make a real commitment to the firm and that you will put your personal plans on hold when necessary to get the work done. They want people who are prepared to roll up their sleeves and get involved, and this includes social events.

Office etiquette

It might sound obvious, but do not forget about office etiquette and basic manners. It is easy to let your guard down while participating in an extended placement but you should keep the following points in mind at all time.

1. Your internet usage might be monitored. Do not surf the internet, access personal email accounts or use social networking sites during office hours.

2. If you are given a work email address, do not use it to email friends and family. Also avoid frivolous email exchanges with other candidates or trainees. Your emails will probably be monitored during the course of the placement.

3. Do not over indulge during social events. It is easy to let your guard down when you leave the office and head to the local bar with some of the trainees, but remember that you will still be watched and assessed even after you leave the office.

4. Switch off your mobile and do not take personal calls during office hours.

5. Do not get involved in office gossip and be pleasant and courteous to everyone around you.

6. It is important to present a professional image so dress to impress throughout the placement. Invest in the best suit you can afford and make sure that your shoes are polished. Also, take care to ensure that your hair and nails are tidy and that any jewellery, accessories, and make up are appropriate to a professional office environment.

7. Send a thank you email at the end of the scheme. This is a sign of good manners and is also a good way of reminding them who you are.

Try to stay on top of your assignments during the placement and don't get too enthusiastic and end up accepting everything that comes your way. Take things that you know are manageable and apply yourself fully, letting the quality of the work do the talking. If you are confused, don't be embarrassed to ask for help or further instructions—it's better to get the work done right and to a good standard. Also make sure that you socialise and stay interested in the firm. If the firm holds interviews at the end of the placement, they will go over everything you have done over the time you were with them so it might be worth noting down things you did across the week, just so you can remember.

Nitish Upadhyaya, Third Year Law Undergraduate,
Cambridge University

16 Pro Bono Opportunities

What is Pro Bono Work?

"Pro bono" means "for the public good". It is generally understood to involve legal work that is being carried out free of charge as a public service. Some universities run formal pro bono schemes, which are often sponsored by local law firms. If your university does not operate such a scheme, you could consider getting involved in one of the activities listed below. Details of other pro bono organisations are listed in the Further Reading appendix.

Innocence Network UK

Innocence Network UK is the umbrella organisation for a body of projects co-ordinated by various UK universities. Each project is run by a group of students under the supervision of a practising lawyer. These groups investigate the cases of convicted prisoners who maintain their innocence but have exhausted the initial appeals process. The student groups review prisoners' cases looking for evidence that might form the basis of an application to the Criminal Cases Review Commission or the Scottish Criminal Cases Review Commission. They evaluate the evidence, carry out research, and prepare a report of their findings.

able skills needed to be a good lawyer. Anyone can put on their CV "I have excellent team working skills", but how do you prove it? The Innocence Project is the perfect way to demonstrate those transferable skills.

Alexander Brown, Third Year Law Undergraduate,
University of Portsmouth

You can obtain more information about Innocence Network UK by visiting its website at *www.innocencenetwork.org.uk*.

Streetlaw

Streetlaw is a programme which encourages students to provide legal education to particular groups of people within their local community. They visit places such as schools, prisons, youth centres, day centres for the elderly, or young mothers groups and speak about legal issues that affect people's everyday lives. This could include, for example, speaking to elderly people about age discrimination legislation or speaking to youth groups about their consumer rights or the use of CCTV systems in public places. Through these activities, you will have the opportunity to show that you can work effectively as part of a team, research legal issues, apply them to everyday situations, and explain them in a way that is accessible and meaningful to a particular audience.

Law in the community

Some law schools run their own legal advice clinics, which provide students with the opportunity to advise clients and help them find solutions to their legal problems. If your university does not operate its own legal clinic, you could consider volunteering at your local Citizens Advice Bureaux or Trading Standards office. You will work alongside trained advisors and lawyers and have the opportunity to interview clients, research particular areas of law, update the case management system, and see how the law works in practice. This experience will also give you a good understanding of some of the social problems that are prevalent in your local community.

For more information on the Citizens Advice Bureaux, visit the website *www.citizensadvice.org.uk*

For more information about your local Trading Standards office, contact your local council.

You could also consider volunteering to help at a Law Centre. There are 56 Law Centres situated throughout England, Wales and Northern Ireland. They are not-for-profit centres that provide free legal advice to disadvantaged people. They advise on a variety of matters such as employment law, housing law, discrimination law, welfare benefits, education and immigration.

For more information on Law Centres, visit the website *www.law centres.org.uk.*

For more information about other pro bono projects, you could also visit *www.lawworks.org.uk*. This charity provides a range of volunteering opportunities to lawyers and law students through its projects which provide free legal help to those who cannot afford to pay for it and do not qualify for legal aid.

Why Get Involved in Pro Bono Work?

As well as the obvious social benefits and the satisfaction that you have made a meaningful contribution to your local community, pro bono work can really enhance your CV. It shows that you have used your spare time constructively and that you have some understanding of the practical application of legal principles. Some of the other benefits of pro bono work are listed below:

1. You will have direct contact with real clients and will need to explain complex legal principles to them in simple terms. This will be an essential skill if you are to become a successful solicitor.

2. You will develop your critical thinking and problem solving skills as you try to find the best solution for your client.

3. You will often collaborate with others as part of the project and thus develop leadership and team building skills.

4. You will develop the skills needed to be a successful lawyer. Depending on the exact nature of the work you are involved in,

these could include drafting legal documents, preparing professional correspondence, liaising with other professionals, negotiating on behalf of your client, prioritising a varied caseload, or legal research.

Get involved in as much pro bono work as you can. It's a great way to develop material for the competency based questions on your application forms. Most universities have their own pro bono societies. If your university doesn't have one, speak to a law firm about sponsorship and think about setting one up yourself.

Jo Pennick, Third Year Law Undergraduate, King's College London

I worked with the Texas Defender Service in my second year, helping research petitions regarding death row inmates. Apart from contributing to answering questions about teamwork, leadership, etc. it gave me a broader view of legal research across different jurisdictions. It also gave me something to address in my interview, and the nature of the work meant that the interviewer was often interested and probed further. As such, because it was something I was comfortable talking about, it made part of the interview relatively easy.

Nitish Upadhyaya, Third Year Law Undergraduate,
Cambridge University

17 Non-Legal Work Experience

Non-legal work experience can be just as valuable as legal placements in developing the key transferable skills that you will need for practice. It also demonstrates your ability to balance academic and paid work effectively, and shows that you are a well rounded individual with experience of life outside the legal world.

> I'm really pleased that I had so much [other] work experience before starting the training contract and had explored other career paths. It meant that I felt more equipped to deal with difficult issues than if I had joined the firm straight from law school.
>
> *Amanda Danvers, Solicitor, Shoosmiths*

Part Time Jobs

The key to getting the most value from your part time job is how you sell the skills you have developed. Think about the skills that law firms are looking for in prospective trainees (see Ch.24 for further guidance) and then consider how you have demonstrated these skills in your work. For example, any role with a customer facing element will require excellent communication skills and possibly also the ability to negotiate with others or diffuse difficult situations. Most part time jobs also involve an element of team working or leadership skills at some time or another.

Marketing experience can be very useful as can any job that involves sales or working to targets. Remember that law firms sell their legal services and time to clients and therefore networking events and effective business development strategies are increasingly important to their businesses. You will also have to get used to working towards fee targets each month so anything that prepares you for this will be invaluable.

> I had a part time job working in a call centre for a bank. In that environment, we worked in teams, we had to reach targets, and we had performance appraisals—all that gives you experience of working in an

office environment and having goals or targets to achieve. It's all good
preparation for life in a law firm.

Rebecca Brown, Trainee Solicitor, Coffin Mew LLP

Placement Years

Some universities offer an optional placement year as part of their
degrees. The value of a placement year will depend largely on the area of
law that you wish to specialise in, the type of firm you wish to train with,
and the organisation in which you choose to spend your placement
year.

Some of the really large, global firms would think that working in a
commercial organisation is more useful and more appropriate than legal
work experience in a small high street firm.

Veronica Oldfield, Careers Consultant & Tutor, College of Law

Before committing to a placement, consider what you are going to get out
of it and how effectively you can sell the experience to employers. You
will certainly gain a sense of commercial awareness by understanding
how a business works from the inside and you will acquire knowledge of
a particular sector, which might be useful for future practice. You should
also learn about effective team work, how to present information at
meetings, how to draft professional correspondence and, depending on
the nature of the placement, perhaps also develop your negotiation skills
and ability to work towards targets.

Students In Free Enterprise (SIFE)

Some universities run SIFE projects, which provide another opportunity
for students to develop commercial awareness and team building skills.
SIFE stands for Students in Free Enterprise and is an international
organisation which seeks to contribute to communities around the world
by engaging students in community outreach projects while encouraging
them to become socially responsible business leaders.

For more information, visit the SIFE website at *www.sifeuk.org*

18 OTHER WAYS TO ENHANCE YOUR CV

> You have to have more than just work experience and a 2:1. You have to be doing something else to differentiate yourself, whether it's volunteering or travelling or any extra things that are not necessarily related to being a lawyer but make you a well rounded person. Anything that shows you can manage your time and balance your studies with extra-curricular activities.
>
> *Rebecca Brown, Trainee Solicitor, Coffin Mew LLP*

Hobbies and Extra-Curricular Activities

Do not focus on work experience at the expense of your hobbies or extra-curricular activities. These are just as important for your CV as they add colour to your applications and help paint a picture of you as an individual, rather than an anonymous applicant who ticks all the boxes but has no life outside work. They are also essential to maintaining a healthy work/life balance and will help you make new friends, reduce stress, and learn new skills.

The trick is to approach your hobbies with one eye on your CV. For example, if you enjoy scuba diving, consider joining your university's scuba diving society and get involved with the management committee. Or, if you love dancing or amateur dramatics, consider organising a show to raise money for a local charity. If you play a musical instrument, do you have qualifications to demonstrate your level of competence or do you play in a band or orchestra?

You can also use your extra-curricular activities to develop areas of your CV that you think need improving. This would show a genuine commitment to self development and a desire to embrace new challenges.

> At university I knew that my presentation skills were not particularly strong so I pushed myself into situations where I would be forced to do that sort of thing because it was the only way I could get better. For

example, I joined the mooting society and debating society although I was petrified! It was a good opportunity to practice these key skills and also to pick up different techniques from others.

A Trainee Solicitor

Most law schools encourage students to participate in internal and external competitions for mooting, negotiating and interviewing. These provide fantastic opportunities to make new friends, learn new skills, boost your confidence, and enhance your CV at the same time.

By participating in activities such as negotiating, mooting and client interviewing, you will get the opportunity to develop genuine legal skills which will benefit you throughout your career. These skills will not only give you extra confidence when you enter the legal profession, they will also look good on your CV. Potential employers will be impressed by students who have proven practical legal skills as well as the academic skills normally associated with a law degree.

Tom Storey, Third Year Law Undergraduate, University of Portsmouth

Travelling

If you haven't secured a training contract and are looking to take a gap year, then ideally you need to get some relevant work experience, whether as a paralegal or in the voluntary sector. However, if you decide to go travelling, you need to show that you have used your time productively. At least then you can show that you are a balanced person who has managed a budget, planned your journey and accommodation, and built relationships with people.

Sam Lee, Graduate Recruitment Manager, Bond Pearce

Ideally, you should get any travelling out of the way before you start your training contract, although some firms offer overseas secondments and opportunities to take some time off just before qualification.

If there is something that you really want to do, get it out your system before you start the training contract because when you start that you need, and want, to be able to dedicate everything to it.

Ben Wheeler, Trainee Solicitor, Berwin Leighton Paisner LLP

I went to the States for a year before starting my training contract. I spent six months working for a law firm getting a pro bono case ready for trial and then I spent six months working as a political lobbyist.

Claire Walls, Trainee Solicitor, Berwin Leighton Paisner LLP

Charity Work and Fundraising

This is likely to be particularly useful experience if you plan to enter public service or specialise in an area of law where you will be exposed to social challenges or where you will come into contact with people at particularly difficult times in their lives. In any event, fundraising and charity work will develop your ability to work as part of a team, to communicate with people from all walks of life, to empathise with others, to negotiate on behalf of others, to persuade others of your point of view, and to work towards financial targets and common goals.

If you are interested in a particular area of law, you might like to link your charity work to that area. For example, you could join Greenpeace if you are interested in environmental law, Amnesty International if you are interested in human rights, or Shelter if you are interested in housing law.

Law Commission Research Projects

The Law Commission is an independent body whose purpose is to review the laws of England and Wales and assess whether they are fit for purpose. Each year, the Law Commission recruits approximately 15 law graduates as temporary research assistants to work on specific projects reviewing and reforming the law. The recruitment process runs from December to January and the posts are taken up in September.

For more information on these opportunities, visit the Law Commission website at *www.lawcom.gov.uk*

SECTION 5: AREAS OF LEGAL PRACTICE

This section is intended to give you a flavour of the breadth of work available within the profession. As you are reading through the profiles of each type of training contract provider and practice area, start to think about what motivates you to become a solicitor, what areas of law you are actually interested in, and what you want from your career. These are all important questions to be answered on your path to practice and will help you to plot your course more effectively.

19 TRAINING CONTRACT PROVIDERS

Law Firms

Many law graduates think they must head for a career with a large City law firm, but smaller firms can offer very good training and will suit some people better. You should choose a firm where you are likely to fit into the culture and which carries out the type of work that you are interested in. The client base and work on offer at a particular firm will determine the experience you gain during your training, your future marketability as a solicitor, and whether or not you are likely to be happy there. Therefore, choosing the right firm *for you* is a crucial decision.

The profiles below outline the key features of each type of law firm:

- **City Firms**—as you would expect, these firms are based in the City of London (although many have a network of international offices) They include the London offices of US firms, the top five "magic circle" firms, and other large City firms. Such firms will have over 100 trainees and focus on high value corporate finance and banking transactions, often with an international element, and complex commercial work. If you decide to join a City firm, you must be realistic about how hard you are going to work and the sacrifices that you will be expected to make.

People say that they could easily do an 'all nighter' but they don't actually know what it means to do three all nighters in a row, or whatever. That has been quite an eye opener in my first seat.

A Trainee Solicitor at a City Firm

Really think about the kind of pressures that are involved in working for a City firm, as well as all the benefits that you will receive. It takes someone with a real drive and an individual desire to pursue success, perhaps at the cost of other things.

A Trainee Solicitor at a City Firm

Passion is a key factor because if you have no incentive to work the hours that are expected of you, then you are going to fall down very quickly. You have to genuinely want to be here. You have to understand that you will sometimes be stuck in the office late at night doing less glamorous tasks but keep an eye on the bigger picture—you are playing an important role as part of a wider team and you must be prepared to get involved. You can't just be drawn by the thought of the money and the glamour or what your friends are doing.

A Trainee Solicitor at a City Firm

- **US Firms**—several US law firms have offices in London and offer between 15 and 30 training contracts each year. Like the City firms, they specialise in complex, high value corporate and commercial work. If you join a US firm, you should be prepared for a tough working culture and extremely long hours.

- **Mid-tier London Firms**—these firms are based in London and specialise in corporate and commercial work, but they tend to be a bit smaller and have a slightly better work/life balance than their larger City counterparts. They also tend to take a smaller number of trainees each year (perhaps between 20 and 40).

- **Small London Firms**—these firms tend to take a very small number of trainees each year and the work can vary from purely commercial and corporate work to private work for high net worth individuals.

- **Niche Firms**—these are firms that have become well known for their work in a particular area of law, for example, intellectual property, shipping, media, family, or employment law. They will probably recruit around five to 10 trainees each year.

- **National Firms**—these are large firms with a strong nationwide presence. They tend to specialise in commercial work (although this is not always the case). They will recruit between 30 and 130 trainees each year depending on the size and number of offices nationwide.

- **Regional Firms**—these are large firms with several offices within one region. They often provide a range of legal services covering both private client and commercial work. They will probably recruit between 10 and 40 trainees each year depending on the size and number of offices.

- **High Street Firms**—these are much smaller practices in high street locations, which tend to specialise in private client work such as family law, residential conveyancing, criminal defence, and employment law. They usually take on one to five trainees each year.

Commercial Organisations

Opportunities to train in the legal departments of large companies or banks are relatively scarce but there are plenty of opportunities to move "in-house" post qualification if you train with a reputable law firm and have relevant commercial law experience. In house legal teams generally have very high volumes of work to get through and often have far less administrative support than solicitors in private practice. You may therefore find that opportunities arise to fulfil temporary administrative or paralegal contracts with in house legal teams while you are at university or law school. This is a good opportunity to make contacts and get a clearer idea of whether this type of work is likely to suit you.

For in-house training contract vacancies keep an eye on The Lawyer (*www.thelawyer.com*) and the Law Society Gazette (*www.lawgazette.co.uk*) and also look at individual companies' websites.

The Public Sector

Crown Prosecution Service (CPS)—the CPS employs around 2,700 lawyers and is responsible for prosecuting people who have been charged by the police. It also advises the police service on prosecutions. The CPS tends to recruit trainees after completing the LPC and generally advertises vacancies a couple of months, rather than years, in advance. The CPS does not necessarily recruit trainees every year so you will need to keep an eye on the CPS careers website for the latest position (*www.cps.gov.uk/working/index.html*)

A typical day for a trainee solicitor with the CPS would begin by checking whether your supervisor has specific work for you. In addition, you can expect to attend court to observe, review cases, carry out research and draft applications and skeleton arguments. You will tend to work from 9.00 am to 5.00 pm—although if something urgent comes up you might need to stay later.

To be a good prosecutor, you need to be able to deal with a significant volume of work, remain calm under pressure, and not be afraid to stand your ground if you have to—you will sometimes be arguing with very experienced lawyers and must not be intimidated by that. You must be an excellent communicator because you will need to explain the law in simple terms to victims, witnesses and judges, and, of course, you must be able to construct a persuasive argument. You also need a positive attitude and can't let the work get you down. It takes a while to realise that you can't save the world and that sometimes you won't get the result you hoped for despite your best efforts.

The best thing about working for the CPS is the diversity of work and opportunity. For example, once you have qualified, you could undertake more training to allow you to conduct advocacy in the higher courts, or you could take on a more managerial role, move into the policy department or consider joining the training unit. I also enjoy the fact that I am making a real difference to my community through the work I do.

Sibylle Cheruvier, Prosecutor, Crown Prosecution Service

Government Legal Services (GLS)—approximately 2,000 lawyers and trainee lawyers are employed by GLS where they advise the Government on a range of legal issues from charity law to constitutional matters, education and agriculture, human rights and health and safety. The GLS recruits approximately 25 to 30 graduates each year who want to train as solicitors or barristers. They tend to recruit two years in advance and will pay LPC course fees and a maintenance grant (although payments will not be made retrospectively, i.e. if the course has already been paid for). See *www.gls.gov.uk* for more information on careers with GLS and the GLS vacation placement scheme.

Local Government—solicitors in local government advise on the relationship between the local authority and the surrounding community and legal issues arising out of the services provided by the authority. This could include, for example, planning law, property law, or education law. Opportunities to train in local government are relatively scarce. They tend to recruit trainees after completing the LPC and advertise vacancies a couple of months, rather than years, in advance. For local government vacancies, keep an eye on the Law Society Gazette and individual authorities' websites. You could also visit the Solicitors in Local Government website (*www.slgov.org.uk*).

I work in litigation so much of my time is spent in case preparation and advocacy. As a local government solicitor, I have a wider brief than the private sector seem to follow, with a wide range of departments using my time. I spend most time at work with clients helping them to achieve solutions to the problems facing our local area—these rarely fit into departmental or organisational boundaries so my breadth of knowledge is pushed at all times. To give you an idea of the breadth of my work, I am currently working on files from personnel, planning enforcement, the ASBO team, information law officers, environmental health, council tax debt recovery, bankruptcy, charity law workers, and street trading! What makes it all worthwhile is the knowledge that I am contributing to making this a better place to live by enabling people to live happier, safer and cleaner lives.

To be a good local government lawyer, you must remember the place you serve and that your role is not to find excuses to say no—your challenge and fulfilment comes from finding ways to achieve positive things. Each victory makes the others working with you more hopeful that they can achieve improvements and slowly we make an area which everyone deserves.

Nicholas Bennett, Legal Services Manager, Reigate Council

I enjoy solving problems and quite often the people who succeed in local government are those who like to get their teeth into a problem and find a solution to it. Quite often this involves lots of legal research and going back to the statutes to make sure there is a legal power for the council's actions. I also enjoy the breadth of experience and diversity of work, and the fact that you never know what you will be doing from one day to the next. But, for me, one of the best things about working for a public authority is that we are delivering services to the local community and if you make something happen in local government, quite often it has a wider benefit for the community.

Sarita Riley, Senior Solicitor (Corporate), Southampton City Council

20 PRACTICE AREAS

This chapter does not provide an exhaustive account of every conceivable practice area; it simply aims to illustrate the breadth of opportunities available to aspiring solicitors. It also illustrates the significant differences between the various practice areas and thus reinforces the importance of thorough research before you embark on the recruitment process, to ensure that you choose a practice area that suits your skills, interests, aspirations, and personality. Although it is sometimes possible to change direction after qualification, you will find it difficult to move to a firm with an entirely different focus if you have not completed any relevant seats during your training contract.

Commercial Law

Banking & Finance

Banking and finance lawyers work on the legal aspects of financial transactions on behalf of banks, investment funds, or large corporations. They are usually involved from the early stages, when they advise on the structure of the deal, through to completion. They are also involved in drafting, negotiating and executing the loan agreement and ancillary documents and monitoring compliance with the conditions of the loan to ensure they are fulfilled. Specialist advice might be required on certain aspects of the transactions, for example tax, so finance lawyers must be good team players and able to take responsibility for managing a large team of internal and external advisors. Since deals will often have to be completed at very short notice, you should expect to work very long hours and must be able to work effectively under pressure.

Commercial Contracts

Commercial law involves the negotiation of commercial contracts including, for example, outsourcing arrangements, contracts arising from PFI initiatives, sale and purchase terms and conditions, agency or distribution arrangements, and franchising agreements. The role of a commercial lawyer is to negotiate on behalf of their client and to draft documentation that reflects the terms of the commercial arrangement. They usually act for a wide variety of clients which could include local authorities, universities, family owned businesses, banks, and other large corporations.

Lawyers in this field need to work closely with clients to understand their businesses and commercial focus, to identify the client's objectives, and to manage any potential risks arising from the arrangement. Therefore, commercial lawyers need to be good communicators who are able to build and manage relationships effectively. The nature of the work also requires excellent drafting skills, an eye for detail, and an ability to think creatively—you will often find yourself putting a client's ideas onto paper without the security of a precedent document to work from.

Commercial Litigation

As a commercial litigator, you will be dealing with a varied caseload of matters. This could include, for example, a breach of contract dispute between two businesses, a dispute between company directors, or a professional negligence claim between a professional and their client. The day-to-day work of a commercial litigator could include meeting with clients to consider a particular aspect of their case and to advise on a next step; meeting with the client's opponents and their solicitors to try and reach a settlement in a dispute; answering correspondence and making telephone calls to opponent solicitors; drafting court documents; reviewing evidence; attending court hearings; and instructing a barrister to provide more specialist advice.

Litigation is a controversial practice area and rarely glamorous! You will meet a lot of hostility at times and your client will expect you to put forward their case in the strongest possible terms, whether or not their case is strong in merit. In those instances, you will need to be able to advance your client's case as coherently and convincingly as possible whilst managing your own client's expectations about their likelihood of success—it is never easy to tell a client that they are likely to lose! You also need to be prepared to act on your feet at a moment's notice and maintain a level head and calm approach when unexpected issues arrive. A successful litigator must therefore fulfil a number of roles—you must be a negotiator, an advocate, an advisor and a mediator.

Being a litigator will inevitably require you to work well in stressful situations. You will often have days where every telephone call involves either a stressed client who needs to be appeased or difficult opponent who wants to make life tricky for your client. Opponent solicitors can make what seems like an easy dispute become entangled and long winded, which makes for a frustrating time.

Never underestimate the number of mundane tasks that also need to be done. For every adrenalin-filled day of Court hearings and urgent work, you will have five days of administration, billing and other necessary, but often unexciting, paperwork. You will also be required to network with other lawyers and business professionals and do plenty of business development work to win new clients. You will need to keep up with training requirements for lawyers as well as reading law journals to maintain your knowledge of changes in the law and procedures. Finally, be prepared for the long hours that you may need to put in where there is a deadline that needs to be met.

To be a good litigator, you must be organised so that you can keep ahead of deadlines and prioritise daily tasks; be able to keep calm in a stressful or hostile situation; be able to think on your feet and sometimes outside the box; be flexible and adaptable to changing situations; be a keen problem solver; a team player and, above all, always maintain a good sense of humour.

Angela Ingram, Solicitor

Some litigators specialise in particular fields such as property litigation, insolvency litigation or social housing litigation.

I work in the litigation department dealing with contentious aspects of housing management and my work includes high profile anti-social behaviour cases; advising on the housing association's policies and procedures; drafting Tenancy agreements; and litigating on all aspects of housing management from contractual disputes to rent review hearings.

I enjoy the fact that social housing is never far from the forefront of the political radar and the anti-social behaviour work has grown tremendously over the last few years. The nature of the work means that you often partner agencies such as the Police, local authorities and social services. In certain cases you also get to see that the court proceedings can make a real difference to the quality of life of people who are suffering as a result of anti-social behaviour.

As with any type of litigation, the essential skills are an eye for detail, the ability to draft concise and relevant pleadings that bring a case to life, a technical knowledge of housing law, and commercial acumen when advising large housing associations on how to spend their legal budget.

Christopher Skinner, Associate, Coffin Mew LLP

Commercial Property or Real Estate

This area of practice involves the sale and purchase of commercial properties, legal issues arising from the redevelopment of land, and issues arising from the management of commercial properties. This could include the disposal of a chain of hotels, the redevelopment of a city centre, leases of units in a shopping centre, or the acquisition of a warehouse.

My day-to-day work includes drafting and negotiating leases and licences for shopping centres and industrial estates; buying and selling commercial properties such as office buildings, industrial estates and warehouses and shopping centres; assisting the finance department in reviewing properties which will provide security for loans; assisting the corporate department in checking properties owned by companies which are being bought or sold (this includes drafting and negotiating parts of the corporate documentation); and reviewing properties owned by insolvent companies and selling them either as part of a sale of the insolvent company's assets or as a sale of the various properties themselves.

I chose to qualify into real estate because of the wide variety of work. The trainees and junior solicitors in the team have their own files and have immediate direct contact with clients when running those files. The ability to take a file from start to finish appealed to me and I really enjoyed this when I was training. I had also enjoyed my finance and corporate seats and liked the fact that, in real estate, I would still work closely with these departments and their clients.

To be a good property lawyer, you will need to be able to work alone and to be organised in order to manage your time efficiently. In other departments you might have one or two large transactions which you will work through from start to finish, in real estate you will probably work on one or two large transactions and anything from 10 to 50 smaller files which you need to keep moving forward while dealing with the larger transactions.

Kelly Myles, Senior Associate, Berwin Leighton Paisner LLP

Corporate

A corporate lawyer may be called upon to advise on a broad range of corporate deals, including joint ventures, private equity and venture capital transactions, mergers and acquisitions, or listing companies on stock exchanges. They might also be asked to provide general advice on, for example, directors' duties or the formation of new companies. Their work will include advising on the structure of a particular deal and drafting and negotiating the main agreements and ancillary documentation.

Specialist advice might be required on certain aspects of the deal (for example tax, property, employment, or competition law) so corporate lawyers, like banking lawyers, need to be effective team players and able to take responsibility for managing a large team of internal and external advisors. Since deals will often have to be completed at very short notice, you should expect to work very long hours in pressurised conditions.

I specialise in corporate transaction work which involves advising clients on buying, selling and investing in companies and businesses, setting up businesses and restructuring them. I work for small to medium sized businesses, family owned businesses, banks and other investors. I chose to qualify into this area because of the wide variety of work involved. I enjoy the mixture of the high pressure environment as a transaction heads for completion and the resulting sense of achievement and relief when the transaction finishes.

A corporate lawyer needs to be very organised, able to process large amounts of information coming in from a variety of sources and be able to pick out key commercial and legal issues from that information. He/she must also have an eye for detail, be able to draft and understand large complex contracts and ensure that such documents do what the client requires them to do. Negotiation is another key skill and linked to that is the importance of understanding what your client's parameters are. It's also essential to be able to work effectively under pressure and accept demanding deadlines.

If you choose to work in a corporate team as a trainee/junior lawyer you are likely to start on a mixture of research, reviewing documents and simple drafting but with experience should progress onto drafting and negotiating more complex agreements, advising clients and even running smaller transactions. Although the work will be enjoyable and challenging it can also require a large number of hours and working nights or weekends, often with very little notice.

Kelvin Balmont, Senior Associate, Clarke Willmott

I work in the corporate department for a wide variety of clients, including FTSE 100 companies, international companies, and some smaller clients. On a day-to-day basis, my work involves a large number of conference calls and meetings as well as drafting new documentation and reviewing and commenting on documents that are already in place. On any particular deal there will always be a team involved so there is also a lot of interaction and discussion with other people on the deal. The job is intellectually challenging and it is very satisfying when a deal is done and the client is happy with the result.

Philippa Chatterton, Solicitor, Freshfields

There are times when you work for 48 hours straight, get in a car to come home, have a shower and get straight back to the office. You can't really prepare yourself for that, but it's a reality of life in a big corporate department. It's not all the time but it does happen. Having said that, I spent 3 months in tax and 3 months in dispute resolution which were much more cerebral, involved more research, and the hours were less intense, but I didn't really like it. I much preferred the team atmosphere of a transactional seat. I suppose the thing is that different things work for different people.

A Newly Qualified Corporate Solicitor

Employment

As an employment lawyer, you will advise companies or individuals on legal issues arising from the employer/employee relationship and the workplace. You might be asked to draft and negotiate new employment contracts or employee handbooks, to provide advice on issues arising out of existing contracts, to advise on how to bring an employment contract to an end and to manage any resulting liabilities, or to provide representation at Employment Tribunals or mediations. You might also be asked to work as part of a wider team to advise on employment issues arising from corporate deals.

Insolvency

Insolvency lawyers advise on individual bankruptcies, corporate insolvencies, and restructuring of businesses. This work could include buying and selling assets belonging to insolvents, advising on corporate reorganisations, recovering assets through litigation, and bringing actions against directors of insolvent companies. Insolvency lawyers need to be flexible and commercial in order to achieve maximum value for creditors often within a very tight timeframe.

I am a partner in a regional law firm specialising in restructuring and insolvency law. I am also a licensed insolvency practitioner. I have been specialising in re-structuring and insolvency for about 15 years, since qualifying as a solicitor.

My practice is focussed on acting for accountant insolvency practitioners, corporates and lenders. As a policy, we do not act for individual bankrupts or their families in disputes with IPs or lenders. I advise on all aspects of personal, corporate and partnership insolvency and re-structuring, primarily in relation to distressed businesses. I deal with all of the usual insolvency regimes, particularly administrations. The practice is a mixture of contentious and non-contentious advice and action, which ranges from solvent re-structuring through to High Court litigation.

The skills required to be an effective insolvency lawyer are quite disparate. A very sound working knowledge of the insolvency legislation is vital. Some of the law is fairly logical but a considerable amount is quite hard to distil into coherent advice and some of the new legislation is badly drafted. Also, a good working knowledge is needed of trust law, employment law (around TUPE), landlord & tenant, intellectual property and real property. As important is a practical approach to the work. Frequently, clients require advice or transactions documented in very short timescales and a good lawyer has to be able to assess what issues are commercially important in a deal. I have, on occasion, been instructed to handle a disposal in the afternoon, and closed the sale that night. As my clients are professional and sophisticated, I have to be on top of my game to win and maintain their confidence. Insolvency law develops quickly with several ground breaking pieces of primary legislation in the last few years, ever changing case law and constantly changing best practice directives from professional bodies and the courts. This means that an effective insolvency lawyer needs to be technically adept and has to take the time to keep up to date on all legal developments. I probably spend on average four hours a week just keeping up to date.

What is great about being an insolvency lawyer is that I have a small number of key clients, where I have developed close working relationships. The ideal is to end up doing a portfolio of cases with the same clients, so you truly get to understand their commercial objectives. The work is intellectually very stimulating both from a technical legal perspective and in terms of understanding commercial issues surrounding business. I wouldn't want to do any other kind of law. I would get bored.

An Insolvency Lawyer

Private Client Work

Family

Family law is an increasingly broad area of practice ranging from legal issues arising out of the breakdown of relationships (e.g. divorce proceedings and the negotiation of financial settlements or access arrangements for children), to advising clients on cohabitation agreements or pre-nuptial agreements, and applying for injunctions in cases of domestic violence. Family law also involves situations where children could be taken into care (known as public family law).

I decided to become a family lawyer because it is challenging and no two situations are ever the same. My work includes divorce proceedings and financial settlements, cohabitation disputes, dissolution of civil partnerships, separation agreements, pre and post nuptial agreements and residence and contact arrangements. To be a good family solicitor you need to have sound judgement, be committed, supportive and willing to listen as well as advise, and be able to create a professional balance. You must also have good communication and negotiation skills, be sensitive and trustworthy, and able to advise clearly and detach yourself from the emotional details of the case.

Oi-Yuyn Wong, Solicitor, Coffin Mew LLP

Personal Injury/Clinical Negligence

Personal injury lawyers pursue or defend claims involving injuries and fatalities caused by accidents at work, on the road, or elsewhere. Lawyers tend to specialise in either claimant work (i.e. pursuing a claim) or defendant work (i.e. defending a claim). They often specialise further in particular areas of personal injury such as clinical negligence, employer's liability cases, or road traffic accidents.

My clients are all victims of negligence and will inevitably have been significantly injured through the fault of a third party, whether it is another road user or a skilled surgeon. They are vulnerable and in need of sound, solid legal advice. It is the role of the personal injury lawyer to understand the client's needs and goals and to ensure that they are met with speed and efficiency.

My clients can be angry, upset and confused with what has happened to them and so it is important to have sympathy and empathy in equal quantity. The personal injury lawyer would not be at all surprised to be acting for any given client for up to five years and sometimes even more. Personal injury and clinical negligence cases are rarely straightforward and require skills in each of the areas taught throughout the LPC and training contract, not least, advocacy, drafting and negotiation skills.

What makes my job worthwhile is to know that, at the end of a case, my clients are confident that they have received a quality service and knowing that those who are most severely injured are being cared for without hindrance of financial constraints.

For those hoping to specialise in personal injury or clinical negligence, firstly, you will need to leave any fears of blood and gore that you may harbour at the door. Secondly, you will need to be fastidious and confident in your advice and when discussing a case with your opponent or in Court. Thirdly, and very importantly, you must be able to explain things clearly and to talk to people who, quite often, are incredibly apprehensive about seeing a solicitor. After all, you're the one who has to make the "No Win—No Fee Agreement" sound simple for the client!

James King, Associate, Coffin Mew LLP

Private Client

Private client lawyers provide specialist advice on the legal aspects of their clients' personal affairs. This could include drafting and administering wills, setting up or reorganising trust funds, and advising on tax liabilities.

My work involves advising clients about their personal affairs within a legal framework, including making wills, appointing people to act on their behalf in dealing with finances and personal welfare, administering estates, setting up trusts and providing advice about different types of taxes and general advice about elderly client issues, for example nursing home fees and welfare benefits. The elderly are often forgotten and I enjoy the time spent with elderly clients and the fact that for them a visit from their solicitor can be fun, rather than daunting. A good private client solicitor is someone who is intelligent with a friendly and approachable nature, a sense of humour, good communication skills, and a commercial mind.

Jennifer Walker, Partner, Wannop Fox Solicitors

Residential Property

Residential property work involves buying and selling domestic properties for individuals. The lawyer's role is to draft the legal documentation, investigate the title to the property and address any defects, ensure that the transfer of funds at completion goes smoothly, and deal with post completion formalities.

I specialise in both residential and commercial property transactions. My residential property work involves drafting contracts for the sale of land and property, approval of contracts, preparation of transfers, investigation of legal title, raising pre-contract enquiries, carrying out conveyancing searches and reporting to clients, completing stamp duty land tax returns, and dealing with commercial lending institutions. My role is to ensure that the process of transferring the legal title to the property is dealt with correctly. If there are any defects in the legal title to a property, my role is to ensure that these are properly rectified or addressed before completion. The most enjoyable aspects of my work are the direct contact with clients and the positive feedback I receive from them. It is also very satisfying to be able to manage and take responsibility for your own workload and take charge from the beginning right through to a successful conclusion of the transaction.

To be a good property lawyer, you must have a clear understanding of the principles of land law, be able to communicate with individuals from all walks of life, be honest, hardworking and extremely organised as you will have a significant caseload at any one time.

Anna Douglass, Solicitor, Brutton & Co

For a detailed account of a broad range of practice areas, visit the practice area profiles in Target Jobs Law (available to download free of charge from *www.targetjobs.co.uk/career-sectors/law*).

SECTION 6: SECURING A TRAINING CONTRACT

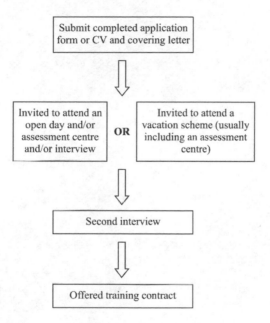

Figure 2—The Recruitment Process

NB—the above diagram is indicative only. Recruitment processes vary considerably between firms and other legal employers. Check individual websites for specific details.

21 RESEARCHING CAREER OPPORTUNITIES AND TARGETING YOUR APPLICATIONS

Students must not underestimate how challenging it is to secure a training contract and I think it's only going to become more challenging. One of the things that they will need to demonstrate is that they are absolutely committed to a career as a solicitor. There is a sense in the industry that we are likely to see more applications from people who would not naturally have chosen law so recruiters are going to be very aware of the need to weed out those who genuinely want a career in law and will be committed and enthusiastic trainees and lawyers.

Sam Lee, Graduate Recruitment Manager, Bond Pearce

When Should You Start Applying For Training Contracts?

The earliest that you can begin applying for training contracts is the second year of university for law undergraduates and the final year for non-law undergraduates. If you are committed to securing a training contract and have sufficient material to support your applications, it is worth applying at the earliest possible opportunity because each application cycle provides a separate learning experience. Even if you are rejected, if you ask for feedback, reflect honestly on your performance, and make appropriate changes to your approach, your applications should go from strength to strength in each cycle. However, do check with firms whether they have a policy on reconsidering candidates who have made previous applications.

Make sure you that you submit your application as early as possible in a particular application cycle. Some firms review applications and make offers as the forms come in, whereas others will not review any of the applications until the deadline has passed. Speak to the graduate recruitment managers at the firms you are applying to find out their policy on reviewing applications. In any event, it is generally the case that early applications tend to be stronger and will have more chance of getting through to the next stage.

Tip *At the beginning of the academic year, make a note of key dates in the recruitment calendar to avoid missing important deadlines. If you fail to submit a training contract application on time, you will have to wait another year before applying to that firm.*

I would certainly highlight the importance of applying early—the firms you apply early to are probably the ones you are most interested in so it does give us an indication of the level of genuine interest. The applicants who apply early tend to be the proactive candidates, whereas those who apply late are probably the people who have left it until after their exams and will spend two weeks applying to random law firms. We've made a deliberate policy decision to process and make a decision on applications as they come in.

Kevin Chard, Training Manager, Blake Lapthorn

Consider the fact that the majority of people submit their applications in the last two weeks before the deadline. If the application arrives in November when the process begins, I have more time to read it without any pressure, whereas as we move closer to the deadline, there is less time to weigh up the impact of particular shortcomings. Also many of the places at assessment centres and interviews will have been allocated already.

Lynn Ford, HR Manager, Blake Lapthorn

We don't act on applications before the deadline, but a lot of firms do so it's worth researching individual firms to find out what their particular policy is. However, people who submit their forms at least a couple of days before the deadline tend to have stronger applications than those who submit later because the applications have often been rushed at the last minute and this comes through when we review them.

Sally Tattersfield, Graduate Recruitment Officer, Shoosmiths

Things to Think About Before You Start Your Research

You should make time for some self-reflection and targeted career planning before you start to apply for training contracts to ensure that you find the training environment that will best suit your skills, academic profile, personality, and lifestyle choices. It is important to be honest with yourself. There is no point applying for a City firm when, in reality, you want to be able to leave the office at 6pm every evening, can't imagine surviving on less than eight hours sleep each night, and have no interest in commercial affairs. Unless you are honest with yourself, you are simply wasting time and setting yourself up for disappointment.

Applying for training contracts can be a demoralising process. Do your research before embarking on the application process. If you do your research at an early stage and build on it, you will make it far less painful and you'll work out the right applications to make. You might think you have to aim at the top but perhaps you would be better suited to a mid-tier firm or even a regional firm and you can find that out by doing work experience or by reading law careers websites and publications, rather than waiting for a firm to tell you through a rejection letter.

A Trainee Solicitor

Your research should involve working out who you are and finding a firm that will suit you. That saves wasted effort in applying to firms that wouldn't actually be a natural fit for you.

A Trainee Solicitor

I was quite realistic about my applications. I was conscious that there was no point wasting my time applying to large City firms. First of all, I wasn't sure I would actually be very well suited to them and, secondly, I knew that my A Level grades would not let me past the first round of selection. Given the amount of time that you haemorrhage on these applications while trying to get a degree, it seemed pointless to me to apply to those firms. So I used the Training Contract & Pupillage Handbook and drew a line under firms of a particular type and narrowed down the remaining firms according to size and location. Also my work

experience allowed me to get a better handle on the kind of firms where
I thought I might be a good fit.

A Trainee Solicitor

Quite often you have vac schemers who know everything that has been
reported in the business pages over the last month, but when you dig a bit
deeper they don't actually know why those events have happened or their
wider significance. This means that they can't really apply this commerciality or discuss it at a deeper level. Part of your research should be
to consider whether you are genuinely interested in business, the City,
commerciality, etc.. If you're not, then don't even start applying to the big
City firms. It shouldn't be something that you're picking up as and when
you have an interview; it should be something that you are always
keeping your eye on. If you're not genuinely interested in these things
then perhaps another area of practice would suit you better.

A Trainee Solicitor at a City Firm

Consider all avenues

Even if you are sure that you know exactly where you want to train, make
an effort to find out about other options and complete a variety of work
experience placements. You do not have to mention them all on your CV
but it will at least reassure you that you have considered all possible
avenues and made the right decision for you. It will also make it easier
to convince a prospective employer that you have explored alternative
options and that your application is based on informed decision making
and thorough research. You will have more to talk about at interviews and
when asked why you are interested in a particular practice area or why
you wish to work for a particular type of firm, you will be able to support
your answers with evidence.

Forget about what your friends are doing and ensure that you make the
right decision for you. You will be at work for a very long time and, after
all the hours of study and financial investment, you should give yourself
the best possible opportunity to enjoy your work and have a fulfilling
career in the long term. It is so easy to follow the crowd into the
traditional private sector law firm training ground but have you considered a career in the public sector working for the Crown Prosecution
Service, Government Legal Service, or a local authority? While this

career path will not suit everyone, there are others for whom it is absolutely the right choice and if they miss that opportunity, they might find that they never achieve the job satisfaction that they are searching for.

It is incredibly important to consider the whole range of opportunities that are available to you; don't just automatically follow the herd into private practice. Consider all avenues at an early stage, including the Crown Prosecution Service, the Government Legal Service, Magistrates' Courts, local authorities, Law Centres, and in-house opportunities.
    Veronica Oldfield, Careers Consultant and Tutor, College of Law

Factors to consider when deciding what type of training and working environment would most suit you.

1. What are you looking for in the type of work that you do (and what do you want to avoid)?

2. Would you like to work on transactions for commercial clients, or do you see yourself working with individuals helping them to resolve issues arising from their personal life? Would you like your training contract to cover both commercial and private client work, or are you already sure which type of practice would suit you best?

3. Do you see yourself working for a large law firm with hundreds or thousands of employees, or in an organisation where you are more likely to know most people who work there?

4. What has motivated you to become a solicitor?

5. What are your expectations in terms of working culture and lifestyle?

6. Which area of the country would you like to practise in? Would you like to work in a busy city or a smaller town? Is commuting time likely to be an issue for you?

7. What hours do you see yourself working? Would you be prepared to work late nights and weekends on a regular basis, or to cancel personal plans at short notice? Do you really have the stamina to

sustain the working hours that will be required by international and City firms?

8. What sort of office culture and environment would suit your personality?

9. Are you keen to take responsibility for your own small client files from day one, or would you prefer to be working on major transactions as part of a large team with little (if any) one-to-one client contact?

10. Think about the structure of training contracts at different firms. Most firms offer four seats of six months each, but others offer a greater number of shorter seats and some offer an entirely flexible training structure where you are exposed to work from a broad range of practice areas at the same time. Which would you prefer?

11. Would you prefer to work for a firm which employs a small number of trainees each year or a firm with a large trainee intake?

12. Where do you see yourself in five and then ten years time? What type of training and working environment is likely to help you achieve those goals?

13. Are you looking for a career with an element of public service and the opportunity to make a difference to your community?

14. Would you like to have the opportunity to participate in secondments to commercial clients?

15. Are you looking for a job involving international travel and/or which offers the opportunity to work overseas for a period of time?

16. Will your A Level grades and degree result limit the type of firm you can apply to?

A final word of warning

It is fair to say that lawyers have significant earning potential, but this should not be your primary consideration when deciding whether you want to qualify as a solicitor and where you would like to train. It is very easy to think that financial reward is the most important aspect of any career and that money will compensate for anything, but this is certainly not the case for everyone. There are some very unhappy lawyers out there and, for some people, a significant salary, and the lifestyle that is built upon it, can become a barrier to job satisfaction rather than a gateway to happiness.

Ignore the salaries. Do not be attracted to the bright lights of London just because the firms will pay you so much more than they will in the regions. Ignore that part of the information that the firm produces. There are easier ways to make money! A lot of people are blinded by the big salaries and don't appreciate the kind of work and hours you will have to put in to achieve that. It needs to be about what you want to do and the areas of law that you think you might enjoy. It's so important to get your research right.

A Trainee Solicitor

Researching Your Options

Do your homework

Your first step should be to review law careers websites and publications such as the *Chambers & Partners Student Guide to Becoming a Lawyer* and the *Law Society's Training Contract and Pupillage Handbook*. These publications provide general guidance on the recruitment process and set out profiles of hundreds of law firms and other legal employers. You can use these publications to find out about the size, client base, practice areas, and culture of individual firms, and to narrow down the list of those you wish to apply to. See the Further Reading appendix for more details.

The Training Contract & Pupillage Handbook was my bible without a doubt. It lists the firms by geographical area and breaks them down into areas of expertise. It also contains information about their recruitment process. That was always my first port of call and then I followed up with the profiles in the Chambers Student Guide to get an idea of what it is really like to work there.

Rebecca Brown, Trainee Solicitor, Coffin Mew LLP

As part of my research, I went through the Chambers & Partners Student Guide, Lawcareers.net, and The Training Contract & Pupillage Handbook. This is useful to narrow down which firms you want to apply for and it also helps you to tailor each application to the particular firm because you can get snippets of information to show that you've done your research.

Jo Pennick, Third Year Law Undergraduate, King's College London

As well as finding out about the size and location of a firm and the work they carry out, you should research its reputation and the retention rate for trainees at the end of their training contract (i.e. how many are offered permanent contracts at the end of their training), and how much choice you will have in terms of the seats that you will cover during your training contract. You will also probably be interested in whether or not they will offer funding for course fees and maintenance during your LPC year.

Once you have completed this research, you should be able to compile a shortlist of firms that you are interested in. You can then review individual websites for these firms and try to make contact with the key decision makers at law fairs or guest lectures. This should leave you with a manageable list from which to start applying for vacation schemes and training contracts.

Trainees can be a really good source of information about a firm, which can help you when it comes to filling in the application forms. Ask them what they think sets their firm apart from other firms and what they enjoy most about training at that firm or why they chose it over others. You can even mention them in application forms to show that you've made an effort to find out about the firm and that you can network effectively.

Jo Pennick, Third Year Law Undergraduate, King's College London

Law fairs

Most universities and GDL/LPC providers host an annual law fair where students can meet representatives from law firms and other legal employers at a single event on campus. These events are useful because they allow students to find out more about particular firms, make contact with those involved in recruitment, and take the first step towards securing a training contract. However, a law fair is only useful if you take the event seriously and put in the preparation beforehand. You need to decide which delegates you wish to target, and produce a list of questions to ask them. There is absolutely no point just turning up on the day and wandering aimlessly around the stands.

To decide which firms you wish to target, you should review the list of delegates and read each firm's profile in *Student Guide to Becoming a Lawyer (Chambers & Partners)* or the *Law Society's Training Contract and Pupillage Handbook*. You should also read through each firm's website. You should find out about the size and culture of each firm; the type of clients they work for and the practice areas they specialise in; the location of the firm's offices; the average trainee intake each year; and any recent high profile cases or transactions that the firm has been involved in.

Try to narrow down your targets to three or four firms so you can spend quality time with each representative, make a good impression, and really find out more about the firm's culture. If there are several people on the stand, try to speak to all of them as they will each offer a different perspective, particularly if there is a recruitment partner, graduate recruitment manager, and a trainee.

The only time that law fairs are useful is when a student has done the preparation in advance. The last thing you want to do is ask a naïve question—you really must know the basics. Sometimes it's a good idea not to start with the firm you are most interested in; give yourself time to warm up a little bit and perhaps start with one that is a bit further down on your list. Always have a pen and paper ready to take down names of people you meet and to note any important information.

Veronica Oldfield, Careers Consultant and Tutor, College of Law

Good research will help you project the image of an informed and motivated student and should also provide ideas for intelligent questions. Try to think of one or two specific questions for each of the firms or organisations that you are targeting. Make a note of the questions on the list of delegates so that you have them to hand as you make your way around the stands.

Do not ask questions which you could answer yourself by reviewing the firm's website, e.g. "what kind of work do you do?" or "do you have offices in London?". Instead ask questions that you really want to know the answer to and which demonstrate that you are a serious candidate who has done their research and is prepared to invest time and effort in their career planning. Read through the sample questions below as a starting point, but remember that this is your opportunity to ask the questions that are important to you.

You need to research the firms you want to target and think about the questions you want to ask. I'm very rarely asked any challenging questions but am always really impressed when it happens. These students stand out as being better prepared and more mature candidates.

Sally Tattersfield, Graduate Recruitment Officer, Shoosmiths

Questions to ask law firms and other legal employers

1. You might want to ask about one of their practice areas or find out more about the type of clients they work for.

2. How is the training contract structured (if this is not clear from the website) and what type of work are trainees exposed to? You might also want to know how much choice trainees have in terms of the seats they visit, and whether any seats are compulsory.

3. Are there any opportunities for commercial secondments or secondments to overseas offices?

4. If you have the opportunity to speak to current trainees, you might want to ask them why they chose to train with that particular firm; what they feel differentiates that firm from others that they applied to; what seats they have completed so far; whether the training contract has been as they expected; what they like most about working for that firm; and/or what advice they would give you in terms of navigating the recruitment process.

5. What qualities are they looking for in prospective trainees?

6. What is their average retention rate (i.e. the number of trainees they retain on qualification)?

7. Do they advise students to study particular options at university or during Stage 2 of the LPC?

8. Do they have a list of preferred LPC providers?

9. How many trainees are recruited while completing the LPC, rather than while still at university?

Questions to ask LPC providers

1. You will probably want to know about the level of careers support that is provided at their institution, and the proportion of students who secure training contracts while completing the LPC.

2. Which firms do they have strong connections with?

3. Are there any pro bono opportunities for students?

4. You might be interested in part time study options.

5. You might have questions about the teaching styles and/or methods of assessment.

Although you might feel overwhelmed by the thought of approaching people at these events, it does get easier the more you do it. You will also find that most people are very approachable and once you have broken the ice with your first question, conversation should flow more easily. Read Ch.13 for more guidance on effective networking.

Take the event seriously in terms of preparation and presentation. It is essential to make a good first impression as you never know where it might lead. A good candidate will appear professional, polished, well prepared and confident (but not arrogant). Do not be afraid to introduce yourself to representatives and remember that a firm handshake and a warm smile will help to project a confident appearance (even if you don't feel so confident underneath!).

Dress codes vary so make sure that you check with the event organiser beforehand. If there is not a dress code, it is up to you to decide what would be appropriate. For most evening law fairs, it is usual to wear a suit but there is often more flexibility for daytime events. If you do not wear a suit, you should wear something smart and take care to ensure that your hair, shoes, and any accessories are polished and appropriate for a business event.

You will know in advance what firms are going to be at the law fair so make sure that you do your research. Approach it in the same way that you would prepare for an interview. Make sure you know about the firm and have an awareness of the type of work that it is involved in. Be ready to ask sensible questions—not just "tell me about your firm"—and dress smartly. We remember good (and bad) candidates from law fairs and I'm always really impressed when students actually email and say thank you for taking the time to speak to them at the event.

Sam Lee, Graduate Recruitment Manager, Bond Pearce

Tips for getting the most out of law fairs

1. Do your research before the event and decide which three or four firms you would most like to target. Write out questions in advance to avoid forgetting them.

2. Arrive on time.

3. Project confidence and professionalism by maintaining eye contact when speaking to people.

4. Avoid the temptation to grab the free merchandise from each stand without even speaking to the representatives.

5. Be courteous to other visitors: do not jump in if there is a queue of people waiting to speak to someone at a particular stand and avoid interrupting other people's conversations to ask your own questions.

6. Treat all representatives with respect: do not dismiss the trainee or graduate recruitment officer in favour of the recruitment partner. In fact, discussions with trainees will often be far more insightful and relevant than those with other representatives.

7. Do not use the representatives as careers advisors. They will expect you to know about the recruitment process, different types of firms and training providers, and to be aware of key deadlines, etc. The purpose of the law fair is to find out more about particular employers or education providers, not to get a crash course in the route to securing a training contract.

8. Take a pen and paper with you to write down important details.

9. Collect business cards if they are offered, make a note of who you spoke to and what was discussed, and, if appropriate, follow up your discussions after the event.

10. After the law fair, reflect on whether you are still interested in the same firm or type of firm. Also think about whether you would like to investigate alternative career or training opportunities. Lastly, reflect on what you did well in terms of your performance, and what you would do differently at future networking events.

22 WHAT ARE FIRMS LOOKING FOR IN PROSPECTIVE TRAINEES?

> The answer to the question 'what makes a good trainee?' can be very different depending on which firm you speak with.
>
> *Malcolm Padgett, Training Partner, Coffin Mew LLP*

> It's not just about advising on the law; you have to be able to go out there and develop the business. We will expect you to have excellent academics, impressive critical reasoning skills, and you must also have something about you in the personality stakes (although that is difficult to define). It's all about building relationships at the end of the day and that is not necessarily related to having a brilliant academic brain.
>
> *Kevin Chard, Training Manager, and Lynn Ford, HR Manager, Blake Lapthorn*

> A good lawyer is someone who is most of all interested in the client and what the client wants from the law, rather than focusing only on the letter of the law.
>
> *Malcolm Padgett, Training Partner, Coffin Mew LLP*

> We need to feel comfortable that we could put a candidate in front of a client. We are looking for people who are confident but also down to earth and who will suit our firm's culture.
>
> *Sally Tattersfield, Graduate Recruitment Officer, Shoosmiths*

Generally speaking, law firms expect their trainees to demonstrate the skills and attributes listed below. Keep them in mind while you are writing your CV, covering letters, and application forms, and think about how you can demonstrate them through your own experiences. However, it is not enough to say that you have a particular skill; you must demonstrate how and when you have developed or used it.

Whenever you make an application, it is not enough to just say that you
are good at something. You must have evidence to support every
claim.

Lorna Sansom, Trainee Solicitor, Shoosmiths

Strong academics

Whatever anyone tells you, your A Level grades matter and you need a
good degree from a respected university.

A Trainee Solicitor

A Level and university marks are important. Almost all firms require a
2:1 degree and most will take A Level grades into account at some stage
during the recruitment process (some even set specific minimum requirements). However, even if you have strong academics, you must not
become complacent and will need to offer something extra if you want to
be considered as a serious candidate for a training contract.

*"Of the 13,622 [law] graduates in the summer of 2007, over half (55.7%)
achieved firsts or upper second classifications"*

Source: *Trends in the Solicitors' Profession.* Annual Statistical Report
2008, p.6, prepared by Bill Cole, Research Unit of the Law Society

Do not lose heart if your grades are weak, but be aware that you will have
to be more flexible and creative when deciding which firms to apply to.
You might also need to boost your CV with some relevant work
experience or paralegal experience to compensate for the weaker
grades.

You can sometimes compensate for weaker grades, such as by showing
you have very relevant work experience, although this is obviously more
difficult in firms where there is huge competition for places. However, for
some firms who state that a 2:1 is 'preferred', rather than essential, there
are ways of presenting your results. There might be somewhere on the
form where you can talk about your grades and show that you were very
close to achieving a 2:1. It's about how well you can argue your case; you
really do need to sell yourself very well.

Veronica Oldfield, Careers Consultant and Tutor, College of Law

Motivation to become a lawyer

All legal recruiters look for evidence of motivation to become a lawyer and a motivation to join that particular firm (or at least an equivalent firm in terms of size, culture, practice areas, and location). The training contract is a significant investment for firms so they want to be sure that you are worth investing in. They certainly do not want to spend money training you only for you to leave at the end of your contract because you do not want to be a lawyer anymore or have decided to move to a different type of firm.

You can demonstrate your motivation through evidence of work experience or because you have been involved in particular voluntary work or projects at university, e.g. pro bono work. You need to show that you understand what it is to be a lawyer and how law firms work. If you have researched your options thoroughly, you will be able to speak knowledgeably and confidently at interviews and show that you have given serious consideration to alternative options and have made an informed decision to pursue this career and train at that type of firm.

Targeted applications and regional links

London firms expect to attract candidates from all over the country and therefore it is less important to demonstrate links to the city. However, firms based in other parts of the country will want to know that you are likely to stay with them after qualification. If you are from Manchester and apply for training contracts in Southampton, the firms will want to know why you want to train with them. They do not want to spend a considerable amount of time and money training you, only for you to return to Manchester on qualification. Therefore, it would be sensible to use your covering letter to explain why you want to train and work in a particular city.

Professionalism and excellent presentation skills

The nature of their work means that lawyers are expected to demonstrate attention to detail. Recruiters will be looking for evidence of this in your application form and during interviews. There are no excuses for poor presentation or spelling mistakes—you only get one shot at this so get it right. Invest time in proof reading your work and ask someone else to read through it before you submit it. In this highly competitive recruitment process, employers do not need an excuse to throw out your application. Also pay attention to your appearance at interviews and assessment centres (see Chs 26 and 27 for further guidance).

Excellent communication skills

To some extent, the interview is the time to demonstrate these qualities but you may also be able to demonstrate them through your extra-curricular activities. Have you had a job where you have had to communicate with customers or clients? Have you taken part in mooting or debating competitions? Have you acted as a course representative or are you a member of the management committee of a student society?

Commercial awareness

This is something that all law firms are looking for. Essentially, it means that you understand how businesses operate and the effects of current affairs/business trends on your clients' businesses. It also means that you appreciate the importance of "fee earning" and the commercial challenges facing the legal sector. Chapter 23 covers commercial awareness in more detail and provides guidance on how you can develop it.

I've realised that much of the training contract is just problem solving, rather than pouring over legal texts, so any display of common sense stands out. They are always telling you to be commercial, which is what clients are looking for. This was made quite clear during my second-ment.

Jonathan Pugh-Smith, Trainee Solicitor, Berwin Leighton Paisner LLP

Commercial awareness is a sense of what is going on in the world in terms of business and knowing that the legal principles do not necessarily provide the 'perfect fit' solution for a client because there are commercial considerations to take into account.

A Trainee Solicitor

Organisational skills and adaptability

In legal practice you will have to balance a varied caseload and meet the needs of several clients at the same time. Effective time management and organisational skills are therefore essential and recruiters will be looking for evidence of these skills from your application form or CV. Have you had to balance paid work and study? Have you had any positions of responsibility that required excellent organisational skills? Have you organised any charity events? Do you have a part-time job which requires good organisational and time management skills?

Firms are looking for people who can balance their studies with other pro bono activities and social events. Equally, if my grades suffer because I've spent too much time organising events or socialising, that will show the firms everything they need to know about my time management skills.

A Law Undergraduate

Relationship building/ability to work as part of a team

The ability to build relationships and work as part of a team is a key skill in the armoury of any good lawyer. Recruiters will be looking for evidence of this from your application form or CV.

You need to be able to manage your time effectively, prioritise your workload, and be able to form good relationships with people because you're often working as part of a larger team and getting involved in negotiations.

Philippa Chatterton, Solicitor, Freshfields

Particularly in a regional firm, clients are looking for people who they like and feel comfortable with. During your training at a regional firm, you will deal with a diverse range of clients from individuals involved in the break-up of a family or the administration of an estate, through to company directors involved in multi-million pound business acquisitions. The good lawyer is the one who smiles and completes their work professionally and really is interested in their clients and their personal objectives and concerns.

Malcolm Padgett, Training Partner, Coffin Mew LLP

Evidence of vocational skills and the potential to be a good lawyer

How can you show that you have the key skills that are required to be an excellent lawyer? You do not necessarily have to have worked in a legal environment to demonstrate these skills, but participating in pro bono work is a great place to start. Can you demonstrate any experience of applying the law to real life practical problems (perhaps through Citizens Advice Bureaux experience or other pro bono work)? Can you demonstrate that you have developed your interviewing, negotiating or legal research skills to an impressive level? Can you demonstrate that you are able to work effectively as part of a team and that you can manage a varied caseload? Can you demonstrate that you are able to operate calmly under pressure? Have you ever drafted legal documents and/or business correspondence? Have you been involved in any negotiation competitions or mooting competitions?

Outside interests

Recruitment partners are looking for evidence of achievement other than academic success. This shows that you are a well-rounded individual and can also demonstrate focus and motivation. Your extra-curricular achievements and outside interests can provide an excellent bank of evidence to show that you have what it takes to be a first rate lawyer.

Enthusiasm and motivation

These qualities could be all that set you apart from other less enthusiastic, but equally well qualified, candidates.

Be determined and stick at it. Show that you are enthusiastic at all times and keep going. But remember that you can't rest on academic successes; you've got to go the extra mile.

A Trainee Solicitor

To make sure that you have sufficient evidence to support your claims, you could consider completing a "map of experience" (see Figure 3). This will encourage you to think seriously about what makes you a good candidate and will save you time when it comes to filling in your application forms because you will already have a bank of examples to hand when answering the competency based questions (i.e. those that ask you to draw on past experiences to demonstrate your skill in a particular area). So many students fail to make effective applications because they do not stop and think about how to sell their experiences to prospective employers. You could have had a host of amazing life and work experiences but that is of no use to you if you do not know how to capitalise on them in application forms and show why they demonstrate potential to be successful solicitor.

Figure 3—Map of Experience

Use the chart below to make a note of experiences that demonstrate the skills or attributes listed in the left hand column. Ideally, you should draw on a different example for each one. Examples could include experiences arising from a part time job, pro bono work, sporting activities, positions of responsibility at university, or participation in mooting competitions. Think about why you got involved in each activity, what role you played, what you learnt, and how and why it shows that you have the potential to be a good solicitor. Try to draw on specific examples, rather than general experiences.

Requirement/Criteria	Examples
Motivation to become a practitioner	
Excellent presentation skills	
Excellent oral and written communication skills	
Commercial awareness	
Adaptability and excellent organisational skills	
Ability to work effectively within a team and take on leadership responsibilities when necessary	
Ability to work under pressure	
Excellent research skills	
Excellent problem solving skills	
Ability to use your initiative when appropriate	
Ability to prioritise/ manage time effectively	
Add additional criteria for the particular role you are applying for	

23 WHAT IS "COMMERCIAL AWARENESS"?

Commercial awareness is a key element of the recruitment criteria of almost all law firms. So, what is it and how do you demonstrate that you have it?

What is commercial awareness?

1. You appreciate the impact of economic, commercial and regulatory factors on the way in which legal advice is given and received.

2. You understand that law firms are businesses too and appreciate the importance of "fee earning" and the timely creation and payment of bills to the success of that business.

3. You appreciate the context within which clients operate and the type of advice they want from their lawyers. Linked to this is a sense of reality about the type of clients you wish to work for and the culture of the particular firm you wish to join. For example, you are unlikely to appear commercially aware if you tell the recruitment partner at a Magic Circle firm that you want to become a City lawyer because you want to help individuals and make a meaningful contribution to your local community.

4. You appreciate the commercial challenges that face today's lawyers and the impact of regulatory reform on the structure and profitability of firms.

Commercial awareness also involves an understanding of way in which law firms operate and what practitioners actually do. Life in a law firm is not just about applying the law. It also involves business development, marketing, networking, meeting billing and chargeable hours targets, client care and client management.

Demonstrating Commercial Awareness

There are lots of things you can do to demonstrate that you are commercially aware. Some examples are listed below.

1. Read a quality newspaper regularly so you are aware of what is happening in the business and financial world but make sure that you understand the history and wider significance of the issues you are reading about, rather than just taking them at face value.

> There are more ways to develop commercial awareness than just reading the Financial Times every day. Also think about reading The Economist or The New Scientist or, if you live in London, read City AM. However, it is not just a question of knowing what stories are covered in the business pages; it is about understanding them and having a sense of the wider picture.
>
> *Claire Walls, Trainee Solicitor, Berwin Leighton Paisner LLP*

> Some people view the interview as being almost like a test so they think they just have to revise everything that's been in the papers in the last two weeks and reel it off and that's it. But I think that's where you can become unstuck at the interview because you might be able to mention something in your application form but the interviewers are likely to want to engage in a full discussion about that particular issue. You probably need two or three key stories that you've actually followed closely and researched.
>
> *A Trainee at a City Firm*

2. Read legal trade publications, such as The Lawyer or Legal Week, on a regular basis so that you are aware of what is going on in the legal marketplace.

3. Before an interview, review the firm's website to ensure that you are aware of its major clients and any deals, projects, or cases that it has been involved in recently.

4. Use work experience to gain an understanding of how law firms work, the role of a solicitor, and commercial issues affecting law firms and their clients.

5. Use non-legal work experience to gain an understanding of how businesses are structured, the impact of the law on the services or products they supply, and the challenges they face within their sector.

6. Remember that clients expect their lawyers to provide timely, cost effective and practical solutions to their problems, not lengthy discussions of abstract black letter law. Show that you can think laterally and find practical solutions to complex legal problems.

7. You could also demonstrate commercial awareness through fundraising activities or relevant business experience.

Commercial focus to me is all about being practical. It's about understanding what your clients want, understanding the markets that your clients operate in, and being able to practically apply business solutions. It's not just about being able to apply the letter of the law; it's about looking at what the law is and how that will affect your client. It's about understanding finance; it's about understanding the sector that we as a firm operate in ... it's so many things. It's difficult to demonstrate commercial focus in an application form although we do ask specific questions to try to draw it out. For example, we ask students to think about a current commercial issue and to explain its relevance and broader impact on the wider market. We also ask them questions about the role of a commercial lawyer. Here we are looking for an understanding of what a lawyer in a commercial law firm actually does and how that differs from lawyers in other practices. It's obvious when students have done their research and are able to draw effectively on their work experience. They need to be aware that being a commercial lawyer is about being a business advisor and building relationships with clients and, crucially, it's about bringing in fees.

Sam Lee, Graduate Recruitment Manager, Bond Pearce

Quite often the question that reveals most about a student's sense of commercial awareness can be something as simple as 'why do you want to be a lawyer'. If a student says that they want to be a lawyer because they want to help people or make a difference to society, you have to wonder whether they really understand the goals of a commercial law firm and what a commercial lawyer actually does. You have to understand that this is a business: we sell legal advice, and we are here to make money.

Kevin Chard, Training Manager, Blake Lapthorn

24 EFFECTIVE CVS AND COVERING LETTERS

How to write an Effective Legal CV

Producing a standard legal CV is fine but it still needs to be tailored for each application. The key is to do your research and to use that research to change the CV slightly. For example, you might change the emphasis on your work experience or mention different modules that you took at university. Certainly, the covering letter should be targeted to that particular firm.

Veronica Oldfield, Careers Consultant and Tutor, College of Law

Most law firms now use online forms for training contract applications. However, some still request a CV and covering letter and you can also use them when making speculative applications for informal work experience. Therefore, it is well worth investing serious effort in creating an impressive legal CV and one that is tailored to the type of firm you are targeting.

At a basic level, a CV documents your education, background and work experience but it is so much more than that if you use it correctly: it allows you to demonstrate how and why you have the potential to become an excellent solicitor. Therefore, do not just say that you have excellent organisational skills, give evidence to prove the point. Think of the CV as helping you to build a case to demonstrate why that firm or organisation should employ you.

What to include in a legal CV

To ensure that your CV focuses on the skills that demonstrate your potential to become a good solicitor, you need to think carefully about what experiences and achievements to include, and how to document them. Before you start writing, take a moment to think about your work experience, extra-curricular and academic achievements, and any voluntary work that you have been involved in. What have learned from each one and why might they be relevant to a future employer? Then use this list to complete the map of experience in Figure 3 so that you begin to link your experiences and achievements to the list of attributes that employers are looking for. Also look at the websites for the firms or organisations that you are targeting and identify the attributes that they value most highly. It is worth dedicating plenty of time to this exercise as it will ensure that you draw on the most appropriate material for each section and that you sell your skills effectively.

A standard CV will tend to cover the areas listed below. You can use this list as a guide when structuring your CV but there are no definitive rules as long as the document is clear, concise and easy to read. Your careers service will be able to provide detailed advice on CV writing and you can also download templates from law careers websites:

- **Personal details**—including name, address, landline number, mobile number, and email address. If you have a different term time address, you should make this clear and state when you are contactable at each address. You do not have to disclose your gender, date of birth or marital status.

- **Education and qualifications**—you should state where you studied and when, and list your qualifications and grades. This information should be presented in reverse chronological order. If you have not yet received your final degree classification, you could include a breakdown of your first and second year grades at university. If you are not comfortable disclosing the individual marks you could give an average percentage for each year but be aware that firms will probably request confirmation of the individual marks at some point.

- **Details of any previous careers** (if relevant).

- **Work experience**—set out your work experience in reverse chronological order and consider dividing it into paid work (i.e. your employment history) and work experience placements. In each case, you might like to use bullet points to make the information more accessible. For each period of employment, you should state your role within the organisation and make it clear how long you worked there. Remember to sell your skills to the prospective employer but do not dismiss part-time jobs just because they did not involve legal practice. The key is demonstrating that you have the essential skills that firms are looking for; it's not about demonstrating that you are already a competent legal practitioner. For example, think about the skills you would need for a part time job in a shop or a customer service call centre. These could include your ability to: diffuse difficult situations with customers; work within a team; communicate effectively; work productively under pressure; meet financial targets; lead a team effectively; and to balance a rigorous academic degree with paid work.

- **Additional achievements or scholarships**—this could include prizes or scholarships at Sixth Form, university or law school, Duke of Edinburgh Awards, mooting or negotiation competitions, selection for overseas placements, fundraising efforts, positions of responsibility such as student council representative or roles within the student law society, and/or sporting achievements.

- **Languages** (if relevant).

- **Interests and hobbies**—mention any qualifications that you have gained through your extra-curricular activities and demonstrate the skills that you have developed. It is better to pick one or two hobbies and demonstrate a genuine enthusiasm for them, rather than listing several activities with little or no detail to support your interest in them. For example, if you have been travelling, you could talk about your most memorable experience or something interesting that you learnt about the culture of a particular country. If you enjoy a particular sport, you could mention competitions that you have entered, or challenges you have been involved in, and whether you raised any money for charity in the process.

- **References**—you should include contact details (full name, job title, address, email address and, if possible, telephone number) for at least one, and ideally two, referees. It is usual to provide one academic and one employment related reference but make sure that you have asked the person's permission before including their details. Consider giving your referees a copy of your CV so that they have a list of your achievements to hand when writing your reference. This will be particularly helpful for tutors who might be called upon to write several references in the same week.

Other tips for writing effective CVs

1. The CV should be clear, concise, and no longer than two sides of A4. Consider using bullet points rather than paragraphs to show the skills you have gained from each experience. This will make it easier and quicker for recruiters to pick out the relevant information.

2. Use a sensible font (Times New Roman or Arial) and ensure that the text is easy to read and not too small. Justify the text and make use of bullet points, bold font, italics, and headings to present the information as professionally as possible.

3. Some people like personal profiles, others do not. If you do decide to include one, it sounds more professional if you write it in the third person and make sure that you have evidence to support your statements in case they are challenged during a subsequent interview.

4. If possible, give specific examples to demonstrate the skills you have developed through particular experiences. For example, if you were appointed to a position of responsibility, give an example of something you achieved during your term of office.

2008–2009   University of Portsmouth Dance Society

- Responsible for organising four events during the year, including the Dance Society Summer Ball.
- Main responsibilities included preparing a budget, identifying suitable venues and narrowing down entertainment options to present to the social committee.
- Main point of contact for all event bookings, which involved negotiating discounts and paying monies.
- Responsible for co-ordinating the sales team and designing the marketing material.
- The 2009 Summer Ball sold 300 tickets—an increase of 30 per cent on previous years.

5. Avoid breaks in chronology; they are likely to make employers suspicious and might lead to your application being rejected if they do not have time to clarify the reasons for the gap.

6. Make sure you proof read your CV at least twice and correct any spelling or grammatical errors and any typos. It is amazing how many people fail to do this. Employers are looking for candidates who care about their work and can demonstrate attention to detail; they do not want people who cannot be bothered to proof read their own CV, or who do so and miss the mistakes.

7. Ask someone you trust to review your CV and give you feedback. However, do not feel that you have to adopt all their suggestions. A CV is a very personal document so it is important that you are comfortable with it and that it reflects you as an individual.

8. Make sure you can actually talk about the things that you mention on your CV and avoid the temptation to embellish any of the details. There is always the possibility that you will find yourself being interviewed by an expert in something you have expressed a passion for. This could be a wonderful coincidence if you are able to hold your own during the discussion, but it will be incredibly embarrassing if you have exaggerated your interest and/ or expertise. Partners and clients need to be able to rely on, and trust, their solicitors and trainees so any lies or exaggerated statements will severely affect your employment prospects if they are discovered.

How to Write an Effective Covering Letter

It is very tempting to run off a stack of standard covering letters in a bid to get through as many applications as possible. However, this is likely to be counter-productive because recruitment partners and managers are skilled at identifying a standard "cut-and-paste" letter. It would be a far better use of your time if you made a few well written and targeted applications to firms that genuinely interest you.

A covering letter is the first opportunity you have to introduce yourself to the reader. Think about how many other CVs and letters that partner or recruitment officer has to sift through—you may only have a minute or two to prevent your application from going into the rejection pile so do not waste it. The letter should explain, clearly and succinctly, why you are applying to that firm and why they should consider you for a training contract or work experience. You must demonstrate that you have made an informed decision to pursue a career as a solicitor, that you are aware of the realities of legal practice, and that your interest in that particular firm is genuine.

The most common mistakes made in a covering letter are:

• addressing the letter to the wrong firm;

• making spelling and grammatical errors;

• duplicating information given in the CV;

• poor presentation; and

• not answering the question—'why us and why you?'.

Malcolm Padgett, Training Partner, Coffin Mew LLP

Encourage the reader to look at your CV in more detail by picking out some interesting facts about your work experience or relevant extra-curricular activities. Tell them about the skills you have developed and why they should take your application further. This is not the time to be modest!

Example:
You will see from my CV that I have been a part time volunteer fundraiser for Barnardo's for the last three years. This role has helped me develop excellent organisational and team working skills as I work with other fundraisers to organise various fundraising events throughout the year. The role also requires excellent communication skills as I have to liaise with members of the local business community to seek sponsorship and generate ticket sales for our events.

Your careers centre will be able to advise you on structuring your covering letter and might even produce standard templates for you to use as a starting point. You should also consider the guidance notes below:

1. Try not to address the letter "Dear Sir/Madam". If you are replying to an advertisement, you will normally be given the name of a particular contact. If you are making a speculative application, call the firm or company and find out the name of the person to whom you should address your letter (e.g. a particular HR advisor, or the Head of Legal, etc.).

2. Explain why you are contacting the firm and what you are looking for. Also state where and what course you are studying.

3. Show that you are genuinely interested in working for that firm. This is your opportunity to target your application to the relevant employer. Perhaps you have completed a work placement with the firm (or a similar firm) or perhaps you met some of their trainees at a networking event or perhaps you have become interested in one of their specialist practice areas since you studied it as an option at university or law school. For local or regional firms, try to demonstrate links to the surrounding area and explain why you want to work for that firm in that area. Show that you have researched the firm by referring to their website or the firm's entry in Chambers & Partners. You could also mention some of the deals or projects that they have been involved in (look the news section of their website).

4. Show the recruiter what sets you apart from other candidates, i.e. why they should find out more about you. Draw out relevant points from your CV and show how they are relevant to this role. If the selection criteria have been provided to you, make sure that you match this discussion to that criteria. As well as explaining why you want a job with that firm or company, remember to explain why they should employ you.

5. Consider highlighting any specialist skills in languages or some other area that you feel is relevant to the employer.

6. Provide a note of your availability for interview and, if appropriate, your contact details for term and vacation time.

7. Adopt a professional tone and use short, concise sentences and simple language. Try to keep your letter to one side of A4.

8. Presentation is extremely important so print your letter on good quality paper and think about how it looks on the page. Format the letter carefully so that the text is not too squashed up or spaced out too widely; justify the text; and use a sensible font style and size.

9. Make sure you proof read your letter at least twice and correct any spelling or grammatical errors and any typos. Also ask someone you trust to review your letter and provide you with honest feedback.

25 EFFECTIVE APPLICATION FORMS

Students often ask how many applications they should make. The answer is as many as you can manage without sacrificing quality and without jeopardising your academic work. You should resist the temptation to run off a stack of application forms with answers that have been cobbled together using standard answers and some creative cutting and pasting. It would be a far better use of your time to make a few well written and targeted applications to firms that genuinely interest you.

Questions in Applications Forms

Application forms usually contain two types of questions:

- **Fact based questions**
  - Personal details
  - Qualifications
  - Work experience

- **Skills based/competency questions**
  - These provide your opportunity to shine!
  - Everyone has to answer the same questions so it becomes easier to differentiate between candidates.
  - Employers will be able to evaluate your writing style and how effectively and persuasively you can communicate on paper.
  - Employers will be interested in how you substantiate your answers and your ability to reflect on your experiences.

Fact based questions do not tend to pose too many difficulties; it is simply a question of completing the boxes with the relevant information. The problems tend to arise when answering competency based questions, particularly when students do not have sufficient work experience or extra-curricular activities and achievements to draw on.

Competency Based Questions

Competency based questions ask you to consider your bank of experiences in order to demonstrate your competence in certain areas.

Examples of competency based questions:

- Give an example of a time when you found yourself outside of your comfort zone and explain how you responded to that situation.

- Give an example of a situation when you demonstrated your ability to work effectively as part of a team. What role did you play and how did you contribute to the success of that team?

- What do you consider to be your greatest achievement to date, and why?

- Illustrate your ability to communicate effectively in a challenging situation.

- Give an example of a time when you had to take the lead or use your initiative in order to achieve a particular goal.

- Illustrate your ability to negotiate a successful outcome to a challenging situation.

The key to such questions is to reflect on your performance in a particular situation and use that example to illustrate the skills you relied on to achieve a given result. Before you start drafting your answer, you need to identify the skill that the employer is looking for and choose an effective example to demonstrate your competence in that area. When it comes to actually answering the question, many employers recommend using the "STAR" model to encourage effective reflection.

We have a number of competency based questions in our application form. Often the students don't actually answer the question or it's clear that they haven't thought about what we are looking for. One model you can follow is the 'STAR' model but so often students forget to tell you the end of the story, i.e. the outcome or what they have learnt.

Sally Tattersfield, Graduate Recruitment Officer, Shoosmiths

Figure 4—The STAR Model

SITUATION (Put the example in context, but keep it brief: what happened/what was the problem/where were you?)

TASK (What were you asked to do/what did you decide to do/what did you decide was the key issue or priority and why?)

ACTION (How did you approach that task? What action did you take and why? This section should document your thought processes and emphasise the key skills that you had to rely on or develop)

RESULT (What was the end result? What did you achieve? Illustrate with evidence where possible)

Other Things to Consider When Completing Application Forms

Preparation

- Print several copies of the form for rough drafts and spend time planning your answers carefully. If possible, keep coming back to the questions over several weeks to see if any fresh ideas come to mind.

- Use the "map of experience" in Figure 3 to make sure you illustrate each question with the most effective example from your bank of experience. It would be sensible to carry out this exercise as early as possible in the academic year since it will help you to identify any gaps in your experience and you might be able to address them by joining particular societies, entering competitions, or volunteering for pro bono work. The earlier you identify the gaps, the better your chances of addressing them before the submission deadline.

- It is easy to put off application forms in order to concentrate on coursework deadlines and revision, but bear in mind that it will probably take much longer than you think to complete each form.

Allow yourself plenty of time to avoid a last minute panic and to make sure that the form reflects your true potential.

- Read the form thoroughly before you start filling it in to ensure that you have followed the instructions correctly. This will include complying with any stated word counts.

Composing your answers

- As you answer each question, keep referring to the individual job specification and the generic list of qualities that firms are looking for (see Ch.22) to ensure you demonstrate as many as possible in your responses.

- Your application should demonstrate genuine enthusiasm for that particular firm and your research must shine through. The best applications will incorporate research in a sophisticated way to add weight to the statements being made, without sounding too rehearsed or clumsy.

You can tell the people who have just applied for 50 training contracts and not really focused on who you are and what you do. A good application will answer all of the questions (and every part of each question), and will demonstrate effective communication skills and attention to detail. It's difficult to do on an application form, but try to demonstrate an understanding of the firm you are applying to. Also try to appear enthusiastic without going over the top. You're looking for someone who stands out . . . you're looking for a bit of sparkle on an application form.

Sam Lee, Graduate Recruitment Manager, Bond Pearce

- The fact that the application is online does not mean that you can adopt a casual tone or that it is acceptable to use text or email abbreviations.

- Do not repeat the question in your answer as it wastes valuable space.

- Good communication skills and a professional attitude are essential for a successful career as a solicitor. Your application form should reflect these attributes. Structure each answer carefully, adopt a clear, concise style of writing, and make sure you have actually answered the question.

You must proof read your applications and ensure that there are no spelling or grammatical errors. It's also important to have a clear and engaging style of writing and to think about how you convey your message. Lots of students write their answers like an essay but it should be more like a conversation. Also, although it sounds obvious, make sure that you have actually answered the question.

Sally Tattersfield, Graduate Recruitment Officer, Shoosmiths

Think about your evidence

- A key skill for any aspiring lawyer is an ability to substantiate your claims. This means that you must provide examples of how you have demonstrated particular skills and attributes, rather than simply making general statements.

More people fail to get through because of the content of their application form than for any other reason. For many of them, it is not that they don't have interesting and relevant experiences to draw on, but rather that they haven't learnt how to sell them effectively to employers.

Kevin Chard, Training Manager, Blake Lapthorn

- Firms are looking for well rounded individuals with breadth of experience so try not to use the same example more than once. If you are absolutely desperate, use a different aspect of the same example.

An outstanding CV or application is one that refers to a variety of experiences and skills—we are looking for individuals with broad experience. We don't want an application form that just focuses on legal experience or someone who uses the same example to answer all the questions. Try to draw on all your experiences and show you have gained something from each of them whether that is netball coaching, mooting competitions, legal work experience, a Saturday job, or travelling experiences. If you use the same example all the way through, you are not picking up any extra points in the scoring process. Show that you are a balanced, well rounded person who has achieved success in more than one area of their life.

Kevin Chard, Training Manager, and Lynn Ford, HR Manager,
Blake Lapthorn

Submitting your form

- Proof read your work carefully before submitting the form. If possible, ask someone else to review it for you and provide feedback.

Make the most of your contacts and get several people to review your forms for you.

A Law Undergraduate

- Submit the form before the deadline to avoid any last minute technical hitches arising from failed internet access or other computer problems.

- Keep a copy of the form for interview preparation.

26 PREPARING FOR INTERVIEWS

You should be extremely proud of yourself if you are called for a training contract interview. Given the fierce competition for places, this is an enormous achievement. It also means that you have convinced the recruitment partners that you have the potential to succeed as a trainee solicitor in their firm. The interview provides an opportunity for them to test their decision, clarify any queries, and make sure that you are as good as they first thought. By this stage, you are more than halfway there and have everything to play for. All you have to do is reinforce the messages in your application and convince them in person that you are worth investing in.

> The magic is in getting an interview. If you get that far, don't even think about being nervous. All you can and should do is be yourself. But do make sure that you are extremely well prepared and have researched the firm thoroughly.
>
> *Malcolm Padgett, Training Partner, Coffin Mew LLP*

> Try and be yourself because it really is a two-way process and you can kid yourself that you will do anything for a training contract but you don't actually want that; you want to know that you can actually work somewhere and that you will fit into the culture at that particular firm.
>
> *Jonathan Pugh-Smith, Trainee Solicitor, Berwin Leighton Paisner LLP*

The tone and format of any interview will depend on the type of firm and the personality of the interviewers. Therefore it is impossible to provide a definitive guide to training contract interviews. The one thing you can be sure of though is that preparation, practice, and personality will make all the difference to your chances of a successful outcome.

What to Expect From a Training Contract Interview

Your interview might be a single partner interview, or there could be a panel of interviewers. It is worth finding out in advance who will be interviewing you so that you can research their career history and current role within the organisation. If you are faced with a panel interview, make sure that you direct your answers to the whole panel, rather than just the person who asked the question.

The interview will probably begin with some "warm up" questions. Do not be put off by the apparent simplicity of these questions. Their purpose is to allow you to settle in and to put everyone at ease before the interview begins in earnest. After the "warm up" questions, the interviewer(s) might wish to clarify some details from your application or they might try to find out more about something that you have mentioned on your form. These questions will then lead into the main body of the interview when you can expect to be asked questions on your choice of degree, choice of training contract provider, future career aspirations, personal interests and achievements, and your potential to become a good solicitor.

The recruitment partners will be looking for genuine enthusiasm and motivation to qualify as a solicitor. They will also want to be persuaded that you are going to be a good match with the firm's culture. The obvious questions at any training contract interview are therefore:

- why do you want to be a solicitor;
- why do you want to work for this type of firm;
- why do you want to work for us; and
- why should we employ you?

You should also expect some competency based questions. These will probably be based on the key competencies outlined in the application form. Use the STAR model to approach these questions (as you would do in an application form) and have the relevant competencies in mind when you answer your question. Try to support your examples with evidence. For example, if you mention your success as a telesales operator, give an idea of the number of sales you made in the last quarter and how that compares with your colleagues.

Do not be put off if there are a few unusual or particularly challenging questions during the course of the interview. The interviewer(s) will be just as interested in how you handle such questions as with the content of your actual answers so remain calm, project confidence and do not let a difficult question fluster you.

Some interview questions to consider

Why us/why you?

1. Why do you want to become a solicitor?

2. Why do you want to work for a firm like this one?

3. Why should we offer you a training contract?

4. What sets you apart from other candidates?

5. What do you think makes a good training contract provider?

6. What do you think differentiates a City firm from a regional firm?

7. What do you think clients want from their lawyers?

Getting to know you

8. What motivates you?

9. How would your best friend describe you?

10. Which work experience placement did you enjoy most and why?

11. What have you enjoyed most about your degree?

12. Where do you see yourself in five years time?

13. Tell me about a current issue in the news and why it interests you.

Some unusual questions

14. What is the worst decision you have ever made and what did you learn from it?

15. Which historical figure would you most like to be stuck in a lift with?

16. Name two of your weaknesses.

17. Which of your characteristics would you most like to change?

18. Tell me about a situation when you had to work under pressure.

19. Tell me about a situation when you demonstrated your ability to lead a team.

20. Are you a good loser?

21. What challenges lie ahead for the legal profession?

22. Are you proud of your A Level results?

Presentations

Your interview might include a short presentation in which case you could be given a choice from a selection of titles, or allowed to choose your own topic. You will usually be given information about the presentation a week or so before the interview.

Possible presentation topics

- Should doctors be sued?
- How will the Legal Services Act affect firms like this one?
- Is there a need to reform the law on assisted suicide?

The interviewers will be looking for:

- interesting, appropriate and accurate content;
- a sensible structure and logical thought processes;
- an ability to keep to time;
- eye contact with the audience;
- effective (but not distracting) use of body language;
- confidence; and
- an ability to communicate concepts clearly and appropriately.

Case studies

You might also be asked to respond to a case study at some point during the interview. The case study might look like a problem question at university or law school where, for example, one of your supervisor's clients calls while you are alone in the office and explains that he has several potential problems that he needs urgent advice on. You will be asked to explain to the interviewers how you would advise the client or what your next steps would be. You will usually receive the case study when you arrive for the interview and you will be given a short time (perhaps ten minutes) to review it. You should also be prepared to comment on any potential professional ethics issues arising from information given in the case study.

The interviewers will not expect candidates to demonstrate significant knowledge of any legal issues arising from the case study. Instead, they are likely to judge candidates on their ability to:

- identify the key issues;

- disregard any information that is irrelevant or which distracts from the key issues;

- identify areas where further information or clarification is required;

- identify and deal with any ethical issues;

- explain the key issues to the panel in a clear, concise and accurate manner;

- demonstrate a logical approach to the problem and an ability to prioritise tasks appropriately; and

- think commercially (where appropriate).

The interviewer(s) might ask you to defend your position on a couple of points, or might even challenge you directly. If this happens, do not adopt a defensive attitude, just be prepared to listen to their ideas, justify your position, and illustrate your thought processes.

Preparing for Interviews

Practice makes perfect

You should try not to become someone different for any interview. The interviewers obviously liked what they read in your application form and the interview is an opportunity for them to find out more about you as an individual. Therefore, over prepared answers are unlikely to be helpful and will probably irritate your interviewer(s) in the end.

It can, however, be extremely useful to attend a mock interview to practise your responses to standard questions and to receive honest feedback on your performance. Speak to your tutors and careers advisors to find out what support your university or law school offers.

Alternatively, rather than engage in a formal interview, you could run through a list of possible questions with your careers advisor and discuss how you would approach each one. This can be particularly helpful because you will receive guidance on what employers are looking for and you can practise using your experiences to illustrate particular competencies, but you avoid the risk of reeling off over prepared and stilted answers. This approach might also mean that you are more likely to address the issues being raised by the interviewer(s), rather than trying to shoe horn your pre-prepared answers into their questions without really listening to what is being asked.

Ultimately it is a balancing act: you want to come across as someone who is polished and prepared, but you do not want to deliver a set of anonymous, scripted answers. The interviewers have already decided that you look good on paper so now is the time to let your personality shine through. They will also be interested in whether you can think on your feet and respond appropriately when you are challenged or faced with something unexpected so perfectly prepared answers will only take you so far.

Mock interviews can be useful if you are very nervous and you're not good at articulating your ideas and need help structuring your answers, but I think there is a danger that you can be too coached.

A Trainee Solicitor

Don't learn an answer; that's the worst thing you can do. Perhaps just have a few points that you want to remember to include in an answer to a particular question. This comes across much better than being over prepared.

Veronica Oldfield, Careers Consultant and Tutor, College of Law

I prepared for interviews by thinking about the top 10 questions and about how I would structure my answer. For each one, I put down the three main points that I would cover but I didn't want to over prepare.

A Trainee Solicitor

Do your research

Your first research task is to try to find out what to expect from the interview. Speak to your careers advisor and find out if they have received any feedback from other students who have had interviews with that firm. If so, perhaps you could arrange to speak to them. Also, speak to your tutors and make use of any contacts that you have made through mentoring schemes or work experience placements. Lastly, have a look at law careers websites, such as *www.lawcareers.net*. At the very least, these resources will offer general advice on training contract interviews but they might also have specific information about the firm you are hoping to join.

Revisit your application form and make a note of the key skills that were highlighted in the questions. If a firm has asked about these skills in the application form, it is highly likely that they are the ones they are most interested in. Therefore, the interviewer(s) will probably pick up on those skills during the interview and take the discussion forward. Re-reading your application form will also remind you of the examples you gave in your answers. Try to come up with some new examples to use during the interview to avoid repeating yourself, and to show the breadth of your experiences and achievements.

Go back to your answers to the questions in the application form—those skills are obviously the ones that the firm is interested in but have some more examples ready and be prepared to expand on the detail that you've already given.

Veronica Oldfield, Careers Consultant and Tutor, College of Law

Lastly, go through your application form and think about any challenging questions that might arise from information you have given. Is there anything in the application that could be viewed in a negative light, for example, limited work experience placements, poor A Level results, or inconsistent marks for degree modules? If so, think about how you could respond to those questions to reassure the interviewer that they should not affect your potential to be a good trainee.

If there is anything negative in your application, think about how you might approach a question on that issue so that you're not concerned about the question coming up. It's quite possible that they will pick on any negative aspects to see how you will react. Obviously try not to be defensive; you need to be as positive as possible.

Veronica Oldfield, Careers Consultant and Tutor, College of Law

Lastly, make sure that you keep up to date with current affairs and legal news by reading a quality newspaper and legal trade publications on a regular basis. In particular, look up any recent deals or cases that the firm has been involved in and be prepared to discuss them in detail. At City firms, be prepared for a commercially driven interview. The partners will want to know that you have a genuine interest in commercial affairs. They will be looking for candidates who can demonstrate depth of knowledge, rather than those who have simply skimmed the headlines of the Financial Times for the two weeks immediately before the interview.

The Further Reading appendix suggests some useful resources to help you keep up to date with current affairs and legal news.

The Interview

First impressions

First impressions are crucial because they set the tone for the rest of the interview. It is much easier to build on a positive beginning than to try to make up ground after a bad start.

- **Always dress smartly for an interview**. You should wear a suit even if the firm's dress code is smart casual or if you are being interviewed on a "dress down" day. Make sure that your shoes are polished, your hair is neat, and any accessories are appropriate to a business environment.

- **Arrive on time** and call ahead if there is any risk that you might be delayed.

- **Be polite and friendly** to everyone you meet—you never know who will be asked to provide feedback on you.

- **Try to project an air of calm confidence** as soon as you approach the building.

- **Smile, make eye contact, and shake hands** with the interviewers as soon as you enter the interview room.

- **Sit up straight** during the interview.

It might be helpful to consider the impression you would create if you were appearing before prospective clients at a pitch for new work. Would your performance put the panel at ease? Would you create the perception of a confident and competent professional? A strong candidate is one who puts the panel at ease from the moment they enter the room, who is dressed professionally, who offers a strong handshake and smile, who pitches his entrance appropriately given the situation, and who is able to engage in the initial pleasantries in a relaxed but appropriate manner. A weak candidate would be one who appears nervous, who offers a weak handshake, who is dressed inappropriately and/or untidily, who fails to smile, who finds it difficult to engage in initial pleasantries, or who gives the impression of a lack of confidence or competence.

A good candidate will put the panel at ease in the same way that a client would expect their lawyer to make them feel at ease. It's about being positive, pleasant, polite, at ease (but not cocky), and demonstrating good judgement both in terms of their choice of language and decisions about when to use humour, when to be firm, when to sit back, etc.. You want to know that someone is calm, sure-footed and reliable.

Malcolm Padgett, Training Partner, Coffin Mew LLP

Body language

Think about your body language throughout the interview. A strong candidate is someone who maintains eye contact, uses body language effectively to communicate his points (without being distracting), and who creates an impression of confidence (but not arrogance) throughout the interview.

Evidence of motivation

Competition for training contracts is fierce and the best firms have the pick of the best candidates. Strong candidates will demonstrate their genuine enthusiasm for the particular role supported by evidence of prior research. They will tailor their responses to the particular organisation and, in doing so, will demonstrate evidence of informed decision making. In short, they will give a persuasive explanation of why they want this role and why they are a strong candidate.

The end of the interview

There will normally be time for you to ask questions at the end of the interview. It is worth taking some time to think about these in advance since your question(s) will reveal a lot about you.

It shouldn't just be a clever question to show off your research; it needs to be one that is relevant to a decision about whether you would want to train at that organisation or not. The interviewer wants you to show a real interest. Don't just ask the question and sit back; try to ask a small follow up question while the interviewer is talking to emphasise that you are still engaging with them.

Veronica Oldfield, Careers Consultant and Tutor, College of Law

After the interview

Reflect on your performance after the interview and do not be afraid to seek feedback if you are unsuccessful. Interviewing is a skill like any other. It takes time and practice to get it right so treat each interview as a separate learning experience and do not give up.

27 PREPARING FOR ASSESSMENT CENTRES

Assessment centres or assessment days are a common feature of the recruitment process. They usually involve spending a day or half a day at the firm's offices with a group of other candidates and allow the firm to see how you interact with others and how you perform in a variety of skills based activities. You will probably find that your first assessment centre is a fairly daunting experience but try to think of it as your opportunity to showcase the breadth of your skills and a good way to find out more about the culture of the particular firm. This chapter sets out general guidance on what to expect from assessment centres and some advice on how to approach the different types of exercise.

Assessment Centre Activities

Firms spend considerable time and money designing their assessment centres across a range of specific competencies so each assessment centre will be slightly different to the next. However, you should expect to encounter any number of activities from the following list:

- Interaction with trainees and partners (usually over coffee or lunch).
- Drafting exercise.
- Individual presentation.
- Negotiation exercise.
- Role play exercise.
- Group exercise.
- Aptitude tests.
- Interview.
- Presentation about the firm from a partner or recruitment officer.
- Tour of the firm's offices.

If a task comes up unexpectedly, try to remain calm and professional. Employers want to see that you can work well under pressure and very often your initial reaction to such unexpected tasks can be just as revealing as your overall performance. You are in the same boat as all the other candidates so think of it as an opportunity to shine, rather than something to be anxious about.

My assessment centre involved completing an in-tray exercise, writing a letter relating to a claim, making a presentation, and participating in a negotiation exercise. This was followed by an interview with the graduate recruitment manager and a second interview with two partners.

A Trainee Solicitor

Group exercises

You can almost certainly expect at least one group exercise at every assessment centre. Firms are looking for commercial thinking, creativity, good listening skills, strength of character (without being overbearing), and an ability to build relationships quickly, to work productively and effectively within a time constraint, to think quickly, to communicate ideas clearly and effectively, to be persuasive but also flexible, to work as a team, and to be considerate towards other team members.

Possible scenarios for group exercises

- You are asked to pitch a new service to a potential new client.

- You are asked to pitch a new marketing brand to the managing board.

- You are given a list of items and must convince the recruitment manager what three items he/she should take to a desert island.

- You are given a list of people and must convince the recruitment manager which three people should be saved in the event of a nuclear disaster?

Tips for group work

1. Make sure that you contribute something to the task, but avoid being aggressive or domineering.

2. Do not be afraid to ask for clarification on anything that you are not sure about.

3. It is perfectly acceptable to challenge other people's ideas as long as you do so professionally and with respect.

4. Avoid being the scribe if it is going to take you out of the discussion but do make sure that someone keeps track of progress, makes a note of decisions that have been made, and monitors how much time is left.

5. Prioritise issues and, if appropriate, consider setting an agenda at the beginning of the discussion.

6. To show different aspects of your character, try to play different roles in each task—facilitator, leader, motivator, etc.

7. Try to reflect on and evaluate your performance throughout the task and make adjustments accordingly. For example, try to encourage others to speak if you think you are being too loud, or try to get more involved if you realise that you have not made any meaningful contributions yet.

In-tray or e-tray exercise

These exercises are paper based or electronic simulations of office life through which candidates are given an opportunity to demonstrate their ability to think quickly and prioritise work effectively. You will be given a scenario and a stack of documents relating to that scenario and asked to create an "action plan". For example, you might be told that you have just returned from a two week holiday and have found the following emails in your in-box:

- a telephone message asking you to call your sister;

- an email from one of the associates in your team asking you to attend a meeting this morning;

- an email from one of the solicitors in your team asking you to take some documents to court this afternoon;

- an email (marked urgent) from a client asking you to speak at their annual conference next month;

- an email from a client asking you to call him about a claim form he has just received;

- a memo from a senior partner asking you to carry out some research for him;

- an email from another trainee asking you to join him for lunch;

- an email from a senior partner asking for information for a new client pitch;

- an email from an existing client asking you to call him in relation to some new work;

- an email from one of your supervisor's most important clients asking you to call him about a new contract; and

- a reminder that you have a training session at lunchtime today.

You must decide what action to take in relation to each document—delegate the work to someone else, deal with it now, deal with it at the end of the day, deal with it tomorrow, or ignore it.

Drafting exercise

You might be asked to produce a letter of claim, a letter of complaint, or a letter of advice. Through these tasks, employers will assess your written communicate skills and your ability to produce a professional document or letter.

Tips for drafting exercises

1. Think carefully about the structure of your document.

2. Sift out any irrelevant information or "red herrings" in the instructions.

3. Adjust the tone according to the type of document you have been asked to produce.

4. Remember that employers are looking for logical thought processes and an ability to write clearly and succinctly.

Aptitude and personality tests

In today's increasingly competitive graduate recruitment market, these tests are often used by employers as an additional filter during the application process. Given the type of work undertaken by lawyers, verbal reasoning tests are more likely to be used in the legal recruitment process than numerical reasoning although some employers use a combination of the two. Some employers also ask candidates to complete a personality test.

The tests might form part of an interview process, or as one of a selection of activities at an assessment centre. However, some employers ask candidates to complete on-line tests at home before the interview stage.

Aptitude tests

Aptitude tests measure your ability to reason (in other words to draw conclusions from particular information) usually either numerically or verbally, although some also test your lateral thinking or problem solving abilities. Aptitude tests are normally completed under timed conditions and generally employers will set a minimum performance level for each test.

Verbal reasoning tests are similar to the comprehension exercises you might remember from school. You will be given a short written passage followed by a series of statements commenting on, or drawing inferences from, the content/meaning of the passage and you will be asked to assess the accuracy of those statements. You might also encounter questions that ask you to look for patterns or connections in lists of words.

Numerical reasoning tests ask you to draw conclusions from a set of statistical data but do not panic if you feel you are poor at maths; you are unlikely to have to get to grips with anything more complicated than basic addition, subtraction, multiplication, division, and percentages. For this reason, it is worth revising some basic GCSE guides to polish up your skills in these key areas.

Abstract reasoning tests require you to demonstrate your problem solving abilities. Often you will be given a series of symbols followed by a new group of symbols underneath. Your task is to decide which of these new symbols naturally follows the pattern and would therefore be next in the series.

Personality tests

Personality tests measure a person's behaviour, motivation levels, values, interests, personal qualities and the way they are likely to react to a particular situation or challenge. In short, they provide a snapshot of an individual's personality and key characteristics. For this reason, they are often used by employers as part of the graduate recruitment selection process because they enable them to assess how a candidate is likely to perform in certain situations, whether they are likely to suit a particular role, and whether they are likely to fit into the culture of the organisation.

Unlike aptitude tests, there are no right or wrong answers in personality tests. These tests aim to build up a picture of you as a person so there will be no pre-determined set of answers and you will not normally be under any time constraints when completing the questionnaire. However, in order to avoid unnecessary stress on the day, it would be worth practising a selection of aptitude tests and personality tests so you know what to expect.

Tips for aptitude and personality tests

1. When completing a personality test, try to answer each question as honestly as you can and, although there is often no time limit for these tests, try not to over-analyse each question (remember that there is no right or wrong answer).

2. There is generally only one correct answer for aptitude tests and you are often under a time constraint (although you will not necessarily be expected to answer all the questions on the paper). Try to keep moving through the questions at a steady pace and, if you are struggling with a particular question, move on and revisit it later.

28 DEALING WITH REJECTION

Training contracts are very difficult to secure so do not be disheartened if you fail on your first attempt. Instead, reflect upon your performance, learn from your mistakes, and use the extra year to your advantage by gaining as much additional experience as possible.

However, you need to be realistic about your applications. If you make lots of applications to a similar type of firm and are rejected by all of them, consider whether that is because there is something wrong with your technique, or whether you have pitched your applications incorrectly. It might be that you do not fit the profile for that type of firm. Reflect seriously on your approach and consider taking advice from a careers advisor or tutor to see if they think you are making appropriate applications.

Some Final Words of Advice from the Experts

Do not give up! If you are sure you want to be a solicitor, keep going and you will get your training contract. However, you must be true to yourself about the kind of law you are interested in and set yourself a realistic goal. Interviewers can tell whether or not your heart is in it. If you really want to do family or crime, don't apply to commercial City firms for the salary alone and then be surprised if you don't get offered a position. I started making applications for training contracts before I started the GDL and made approximately 50 applications over three years. I was confident that I would secure a training contract as I had good grades and, as a more mature student, I had plenty of life/work/client experience. However, I made a serious mistake—I was not honest with myself about the type of firm I wanted to work for. I only applied to large firms with huge salaries who specialised in corporate law. I had many interviews but was rejected each time. I could not understand why and began to lose confidence. After I finished the LPC, I stopped worrying about salary and made a few well researched and well considered applications to firms I was genuinely interested in. I interviewed at one particular firm that I was very excited about and where I could see myself being very happy. I found it remarkable that I could be myself at the interview and did not need to feign an interest in corporate law, or pretend that I read the Financial Times every day. I was very comfortable during the recruitment process and I actually quite enjoyed the assessment day and the interview. I felt instantly 'at home' and was delighted to be offered a training contract. In hindsight, I am extremely pleased that I did not get offered a training contract with any of the firms I applied to initially. I have no interest in corporate law and I am not surprised that the interviewers could see that.

A Trainee Solicitor

If you are consistently failing to get through the first stage of the application process, it's absolutely crucial to get some feedback. If you don't know where you are going wrong, you won't know how to improve and you might be making the same mistake time and time again. It might be something that you can rectify quite easily.

A Graduate Recruitment Manager

If you are getting assessment centres but not getting any further than that, you need to think seriously about what you are doing wrong and the best way to do this is to ask for some feedback from firms.

A Graduate Recruitment Manager

I applied for training contracts during my second year at university but didn't get anywhere so I reapplied in my third year and found that my applications were far more successful, possibly because, on reflection, the first time round I applied to firms that I wouldn't actually have wanted to work for. My applications were far more targeted second time round. I had also volunteered to help at the university's listening service and I had completed three vacation schemes so I had a lot more on my CV second time round.

A Trainee Solicitor

If you know that you really want to become a solicitor, just keep trying. Maybe the right firm finds you in the end and those rejections are just part of the process of sifting out the ones where you wouldn't actually be happy in the long term.

A Trainee Solicitor

APPENDIX 1

MONEY MATTERS

Qualifying as a solicitor is an expensive undertaking. Fees for the LPC alone can be up to £12,500. If you add to that the cost of completing a law degree, or non-law degree and GDL, plus living expenses throughout your studies, you will get an idea of the level of financial investment that is involved.

Some firms fund the cost of the LPC for their trainees and others will fund both the LPC and GDL for any non-law graduates in their trainee intake. However, for many aspiring solicitors the cost of qualification must be borne privately since, unlike university studies, you are unlikely to receive any funding from your local education authority. This appendix outlines a selection of funding sources, but your careers department might be able to suggest others.

Law School Scholarships and Bursaries

Some law schools offer scholarships, which usually take the form of a reduction in fees, rather than a cash award. They might also offer limited bursaries for students who are struggling to meet the costs of the course. Contact your provider for further details.

Law Society Schemes

Law Society Bursary Scheme

This scheme supports the development of individuals who can demonstrate exceptional academic ability and potential as a solicitor. Applicants can apply for any amount up to the total cost of their course fees, but must have a confirmed place on the LPC course before they submit their application.

Law Society Diversity Access Scheme

The Diversity Access Scheme supports individuals who must overcome exceptional obstacles to qualify as a solicitor. The scheme provides funding to cover LPC course fees.

210 Appendix 1

For more information on these schemes, visit *http://juniorlawyers.law society.org.uk/node/140*.

Other Awards and Scholarships

Legal Services Commission (LSC) Training Contract Grants Scheme

Since 2002, the LSC has been awarding Training Contract Grants to organisations committed to legal aid work. The aim of these grants is to support organisations in recruiting and retaining legal aid lawyers. Each grant represents a commitment to support a student/trainee and an organisation for up to four years, including a contribution to LPC course fees and salary costs.

For more information about this scheme, go to *www.legalservices.gov .uk/public/training_contract_grants.asp*.

HRLA Bursary Award 2008

The Human Rights Lawyers' Association (HRLA) bursary scheme enables law students to undertake work placements in the field of human rights. In 2009, the HRLA offered between three and five awards from a maximum bursary fund of £5,000. Single awards do not normally amount to more than £1,000.

For more information on this scheme, go to *www.hrla.org.uk/Bursary_ 2009.php*.

The Inderpal Rahal Memorial Trust

The Inderpal Rahal Memorial Trust makes one, or occasionally two, awards of £2,000 per year towards legal training for women from an immigrant or refugee background who intend to practise or teach law in the UK. Candidates are required to complete an application form and those shortlisted will be asked to attend an interview. You should note, however, that awards will not be made to those taking a first degree in law.

Contact the trust administrator for further details, either by email *irmt@gclaw.co.uk*, or by writing to:

Inderpal Rahal Memorial Trust
Garden Court Chambers
57–60 Lincoln's Inn Fields
London WC2A 3LJ

Charities and Grant-Making Trusts

Contact your LEA awards officer and ask for information about local charities and any grant-making trusts for which you may qualify. Qualifications for these awards vary enormously and they usually provide only small amounts of money.

The Trainee Solicitors Group provides some useful information on funding and scholarships at *www.tsg.org/scholarships.html*.

Discretionary Local Educational Authority (LEA) Awards

Some LEAs offer awards for people who are starting professional courses. However, awards for the LPC and GDL are discretionary and awards are limited. Your LEA will be able to provide you with details of its discretionary award policies.

Professional and Career Development Loans

These are specialist bank loans which can relieve financial pressure while you study. Interest rates tend to be competitive but you will need to consider whether you will be in a position to repay the loan if you have not secured a training contract by the time you finish the LPC.

NB—Professional and Career Development Loans are not available to fund the GDL.

For more information on Professional and Career Development Loans, go to *www.direct.gov.uk/cdl* or call 0800 585 505 or contact banks directly.

Bank Loans

This is an expensive, but for many students inevitable, source of funding. Make sure you research your options carefully before entering into a loan agreement to ensure you choose the most competitive option and are aware of your obligations and liabilities under the agreement.

Bank Overdraft

Some banks provide an interest free overdraft facility for students, but this will only cover a fairly small proportion of the GDL/LPC fees, and interest will become payable eventually.

Part Time Study

Some providers offer part time study routes for the GDL and LPC. This can be a useful option for some students as it allows them to combine their studies with paid work.

Delay Study

If you are funding your studies privately, you could consider taking a year or two out before starting the LPC so you can save money to pay your course fees and living expenses. Working as a paralegal is a useful option because it allows you to gain legal work experience while building up your savings.

APPENDIX 2

FURTHER READING AND OTHER RESOURCES

The following list is to help you locate further information. The contact details and web addresses were correct at the time of going to press.

Professional and Regulatory Bodies

The Law Society.
The Law Society's Hall.
113 Chancery Lane.
London WC2A 1PL.
020 7242 1222.
www.lawsociety.org.uk.

Solicitors Regulation Authority.
Ipsley Court.
Berrington Close.
Redditch.
B98 0TD.
0870 606 2555.
www.sra.org.uk.

Legal Directories

Chambers & Partners UK Guide—this directory is also available at: *www.chambersandpartners.com.*
The Legal 500—this directory is also available at *www.legal500.com.*

Legal Careers Publications and Training Contract Listings

The following publications are distributed to students free of charge through their law school or university law department. Alternatively, they can be purchased from a legal bookshop or accessed online.

Chambers Student: The Student's Guide to Becoming a Lawyer (Chambers & Partners)—this guide is also available at *www.chambers student.co.uk*.

Target Law—this guide is also available at *www.targetjobs.co.uk/career-sectors/law*.

The Training Contract and Pupillage Handbook (in association with The Trainee Solicitor Group)—this guide is also available at *www.tcph.co.uk*.

Books for Law Students and Aspiring Law students

C. Barnard, J. O'Sullivan & G. Virgo, *What about Law?*, (Hart Publishing, 2007).

S. Foster, *How to Write Better Law Essays*, (2nd edn, Longman, 2009).

N. J. McBride, *Letters to a Law Student*, (Pearson, 2007).

G. Williams, *Learning the Law*, (13th edn, Sweet & Maxwell, 2006).

S. Wilson & P. Kenny, *The Law Student's Handbook* (Oxford University Press, 2007).

Books on Preparing for Interviews

M. Eggert, *Perfect Interview*, (Random House Books, 2008).

M. Eggert, *Perfect Answers to Interview Questions*, (Random House Books, 2007).

Books on Preparing for the LNAT

R. Hutton, G. Hutton & F. Simpson, *Passing the National Admissions Test for Law* (2nd edn, Law Matters Publishing, 2008).

M. Shepherd, *Mastering the National Admissions Test for Law* (Routledge Cavendish, 2005).

Useful Websites

Training Related Websites

www.lawcabs.ac.uk—the central applications website for the GDL and LPC.

www.lifelonglearning.co.uk/cdl—career development loans.
www.ucas.com—the central organisation for applying to universities in the UK.

Legal Careers Websites

www.allaboutlaw.co.uk—All About Law—a relatively new legal careers website, which aims to de-mystify the legal profession and the recruitment process. The site features blogs from current trainees and law students and some useful information for pre-university students who are interested in a legal career.
www.chambersstudent.co.uk—Chambers & Partners Student Guide to Becoming a Lawyer—a comprehensive source of information on legal careers and the recruitment process, including a detailed database of law firms, useful timetables for vacation scheme and training contract applications, and an explanation of key practice areas.
www.lawcareers.net—Law Careers—a comprehensive source of information on legal careers and the recruitment process, including interviews with recruiters and trainees, legal news, and an explanation of key practice areas.
www.prospects.ac.uk/p/sectors/law_sector.jsp—Prospects Law—general information about the legal profession and careers advice.
www.targetjobs.co.uk/law—Target Jobs Law—you can download a copy of the Target Law magazine from this site. The publication is a comprehensive source of information on legal careers and the recruitment process. It includes useful advice on completing application forms and preparing for interviews and assessment centres, and has some interesting case studies on LPC students and trainee solicitors.

Legal Trade Publications

www.lawgazette.co.uk—the Law Society's Gazette with news and jobs aimed at solicitors.
www.legalweek.com—online legal magazine featuring legal news and information.
www.thelawyer.com—online legal magazine featuring legal news and information.
www.thelawyer.com/l2b—the student website attached to *The Lawyer*.

General Legal Interest

www.cityam.com—the online version of the free daily London business newspaper.

www.lawcrossing.co.uk—a subscription service offering legal jobs including paralegal positions and vacation work.

www.rollonfriday.com—a light-hearted site featuring news and gossip on the legal profession and aimed primarily at solicitors and aspiring solicitors.

www.timesonline.co.uk/law—*The Times* Law Section.

Charities and Other Organisations with Volunteering Opportunities

www.ageconcern.org.uk/AgeConcern/mhap.asp—Age Concern Mental Capacity Advocacy Project—volunteer advocacy for older people who lack mental capacity.

www.amicus-alj.org—Amicus, assisting lawyers for justice on Death Row.

www.amnesty.org.uk—Amnesty International—worldwide human rights campaign group.

www.appropriateadult.org.uk—National Appropriate Adult Network —providing an 'appropriate adult' for those under the age of 17 and adults who are considered to be mentally vulnerable during police interviews.

www.biduk.org—Bail for Immigration Detainees (BID)—an independent charity seeking to challenge immigration detention in the UK.

www.citizensadvice.org.uk—the CAB website.

www.community-links.org/local-services/advice—Community Links Advice Team, local charity in East London which includes advice on welfare benefits, housing and debt, and employment law, private housing and consumer law.

www.dls.org.uk—Disability Law Service, providing advice to disabled and deaf people.

www.dsc.org.uk—the Directory of Social Change, information about working in the voluntary sector.

www.freerepresentationunit.org.uk—the Free Representation Unit (FRU), providing free legal representation for Employment Tribunals, Social Security appeals in the Social Security and Child Support Appeals

Tribunals and some immigration and criminal injury compensation cases.

www.howardleague.org—The Howard League for Penal Reform, the oldest penal reform charity in the UK.

www.iasuk.org—Immigration Advisory Service, advice and representation in immigration and asylum law.

www.innocencenetwork.org.uk—Innocence Network UK (INUK).

www.justice.org.uk—Justice, the human rights organisation.

www.lawcentres.org.uk—the Law Centres Federation, not-for-profit legal practices offering free legal advice and representation to disadvantaged people.

www.lawworks.org.uk—LawWorks, a charity providing free legal help to individuals and community groups who cannot afford to pay for it and cannot access legal aid.

www.liberty-human-rights.org.uk—Liberty, the human rights organisation.

www.reprieve.org.uk—Reprieve—fighting for people on Death Row.

www.sifeuk.org—Students In Free Enterprise (SIFE).

www.star-network.org.uk—Student Action for Refugees (STAR), a national network of student groups working to improve the lives of refugees in the UK.

www.tradingstandards.gov.uk—the Trading Standards Institute website.

www.victimsupport.org.uk—Victim Support, national charity for victims and witnesses of crime in England and Wales.

Other Useful Organisations and Special Interest Groups

www.aml.org.uk—The Association of Muslim Lawyers.

www.armylegal.co.uk—Army Legal Services.

www.blacksolicitorsnetwork.co.uk—Black Solicitors Network.

www.cps.gov.uk—the Crown Prosecution Service (CPS).

www.dca.gov.uk—the Department of Constitutional Affairs (now known as the Ministry of Justice) archived webpage.

www.gls.gov.uk—Government Legal Services (GLS).

www.justice.gov.uk—the Ministry of Justice.

www.lapg.co.uk—the Legal Aid Practitioners Group.

www.lawcf.org—the Lawyers' Christian Fellowship.

www.lawsociety.org.uk/lawyerswithdisabilities—the Law Society Lawyers with Disabilities Group.

www.lawsociety.org.uk/juniorlawyers—the Law Society Junior Lawyers Division.
www.magistrates-association.org.uk—the Magistrates' Association.
www.raf.mod.uk/legalservices—Royal Air Force (RAF) Legal Services.
www.slgov.org.uk—Solicitors in Local Government.
www.societyofasianlawyers.org—the Society of Asian Lawyers.
www.womensolicitors.org.uk—the Association of Women Solicitors.